The *Cross Stitch* House

The Cross Stitch House

Melinda Coss

ANAYA PUBLISHERS LTD
LONDON

For David and Nest Rubio,
both of whom I love dearly

First published in Great Britain in 1994 by
Anaya Publishers Ltd, Strode House,
44-50 Osnaburgh Street, London NW1 3ND

Managing editor   Jane Struthers
Design   Peartree Design Associates
Charts and diagrams   Steve Dew and Delia Elliman
Photography   Di Lewis
Detail photography   J A Ducker

British Library Cataloguing in Publication Data

Coss, Melinda
Cross-stitch House
I. Title
746.44

ISBN 1-85470-173-8

Typeset in Great Britain by Litho Link Ltd, Welshpool, Powys
Colour reproduction by Scantrans Pte Ltd, Singapore
Printed and bound by Dai Nippon in Hong Kong

Contents

INTRODUCTION

Our choice in home decoration is influenced by numerous factors. Personal taste, our sex, the character of the building, the sizes and ages of our families, practicality, expense, fashion and, last but not least, the amount/style of furnishings we need to incorporate from past times and different places all have to be considered.

Faced with finding solutions for all these considerations and having moved nine times in my adult life, the last time I did it I was sorely tempted to leave all the rooms of my new home undecorated and unfurnished as a statement of my personal mobility . . . and would have done so if only I could have handled the trauma of parting with treasured pre-war editions of *Vogue*, rusting milk churns, super-duper, high-tech vegetable chopper-uppers, my children's old school paintings, 45 soft toys all with their own names and stories to tell and those antique weighing scales that seem to have attached themselves to me over the years.

Then of course there are all those wonderful magazines telling me how rewarding craft work is and that as a homemaker of the 1990s I need to learn how to 'distress' my extremely expensive and smooth plaster finishes, how to drape my curtains (what curtains?) and how to turn my milk churn into a piece of art. My beautiful copper pipes should be painted verdigris to make them look as if they are leaking but, while it is highly desirable to own an original cooking range, I really should forget about the coal and

wood and change to oil or gas . . .

My reaction to these mixed messages is 'compromise'. It is important that my home has individuality and style but I am not prepared to destroy perfectly good walls to achieve it. If my timber is

already curling at the edges then all well and good – it has accomplished 1990s fashion status all by itself. My leanings, however (and hopefully yours too or you wouldn't be reading this book), are toward needle and thread, and with needle

and thread I will decorate, emphasize, interpret and enjoy those valuable bits of nostalgia that are now so much a part of me.

If you are making a new home, this book will give you the means to begin your own collection of treasures in cross stitch. If, like me, your past inspirations travel with you, it is really a question of re-grouping what is in danger of becoming junk and accessorizing it with your cross stitch skills so that a theme for a particular room becomes apparent and your personal signature is clearly stated. There is no reason on earth why a house should be decorated in one all-over style, be it classical or modern. A home should spell out the personalities of the people living in it and, provided you take colour schemes into account, there is no reason why classical and modern decorations cannot work in harmony. If you are comfortable with clutter but have a super-tidy partner, establish space for both: a cosy cluttered bedroom and a Japanese-style living room could well offer the solution to your problems.

If you have children, use your needle and thread to create environments for them which will not only be individual and stimulating but will, I guarantee, remain in their memories throughout adulthood.

When you begin to look around your room with a cross stitcher's eye, numerous items will present

themselves to you for decoration. Those plain curtains, that tablecloth . . . just think carefully and use your skills to co-ordinate items so that they provide their own overall look.

For cross stitch beginners, this book will hopefully introduce you to a rewarding and therapeutic skill that is simple to achieve. The techniques section describes a relaxed approach to cross stitch and the projects are designed to inspire you with new and interesting items which can be worked using almost any of the supplied charts.

Do not feel restricted by my choice of colours – you should select colours which fit in with your own scheme of things. Since recycling is important in this day and age, make use of the bits and bobs around you and use your flair and imagination to give them a new lease of life. If you are making a home on a tight budget, don't spend money on fancy linens and bedding, go for plain colours which are usually considerably cheaper and decorate them with cross stitch.

While my earlier comments

might suggest that I am a little bemused by paint finishes that are designed to age your home, I am all in favour of stencilling and freestyle painting, both of which can add immense character to a room. You can adapt stencil designs into cross stitch charts and vice versa, so treat the designs available to you in their broadest possible terms. Because something is intended for tapestry,

that doesn't mean it can't be used for anything else and it will probably work beautifully in cross stitch. Experiment!

I won't keep you any longer because I want you to get started, but one word of warning – cross stitch is addictive and you might just end up needing to move to a larger house . . .

MELINDA COSS

Page 7: *Spring Bouquet Heart and Little Lace Heart.* Facing page: *Delft Napkin and Delft Tablecloth.*
Left: *Japanese Lampshade; Japanese Paperweight; Japanese Sunrise Bookmark; Japanese Address Book; Playing Card Glasses Case; Bridge Pad.*
Above: *Cupid on Paper Canvas.*

Kitchens

THE DELFT KITCHEN

There has been a great rise in the popularity of blue and white porcelain and earthenware, and many original pieces are now used decoratively to brighten up a kitchen dresser. Delftware designs have also been used as inspiration for wall tiles because the simple colour scheme of cobalt blue on white adds character and charm to a basic kitchen.

Delftware originated in Holland where it served the purpose of 'poor man's porcelain'. It was, however, a source of grief to the eighteenth-century Dutch housewife since the white tin glaze tended to chip off the underlying clay body. It is ironic to think that many of the domestic items we seek out and treasure today served as a great burden to those who had to use, clean and care for them in the past.

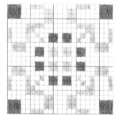

Delft Clock

Kitchen, bathroom and fireplace tiles provide a wonderful source of inspiration and can easily be translated into attractive cross stitch designs. The regular shape of the tile and the use of geometric and mirror images makes the motifs suitable for a large number of projects since you can add and remove tile shapes to build up different sized blocks and borders. For example, in this section, I have made up a clock, a tablecloth, a pot holder and a napkin, all based on the designs of Delft tiles. You might choose to make a frieze for a blind (window shade) or to use the square motifs for a picture frame or book cover.

Producing your basic design is simple. You could either trace an image directly from a tile on to graph paper or, if you have a spare tile, you can photocopy it and then either enlarge or reduce it to your required size before tracing the image on the paper.

Actual design measures:
13 in (33 cm) square

Materials
1 piece of 14-count Aida, in white, measuring approximately 17 in (43 cm) square
No 7 crewel needle
A piece of hardboard (masonite) or stiff cardboard measuring 13 in (33 cm) square
Rubber-based adhesive
Quartz clock movement and set of hands, with the big hand measuring 3½ in (8.9 cm)
Scalpel or craft knife

Anchor stranded cottons (floss):

 4 skeins of light blue (130)

3 skeins of dark blue (131)

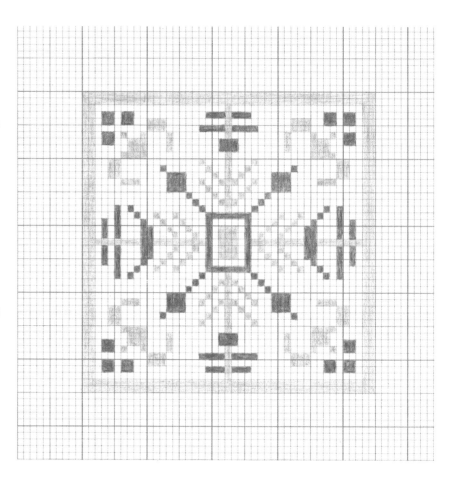

Instructions
I have allowed 1 in (2.5 cm) of selvedge (selvage) at each edge so, if you choose to begin at, say, the bottom right hand corner, start stitching on the 14th hole in from the right edge and the 14th hole up from the bottom edge and work the outside borders made up from large tiles first. Note that the tiles are joined horizontally with two rows of stitching instead of four.

Work the design entirely in cross stitch, using three strands of cotton (floss). Having worked the eight large border motifs, complete the horizontal bands of small motifs and then position the large tile motif that supports the clock hands by finding the centre of both the fabric and the design and working from that point. Finally, position and stitch the numbers for the clock face.

Finishing
When your design is complete, lay your fabric, right side up, square on your piece of hardboard (masonite) or cardboard. Fold the selvedges (selvages) carefully to the back of the cardboard, turn your work face down and glue the edges in place, taking care to keep your design square.

With the scalpel or craft knife, carefully cut the threads in the middle of the centre tile so you can insert the clock hand support. If you are using cardboard as a backing you can make a hole by pushing a knitting needle through this central gap. If you are using hardboard, a small hand drill will do the trick. Fix the clock works in position following the manufacturer's instructions.

Delft Napkin

To complete the look for your blue and white kitchen, you can add a small motif to a set of matching napkins. Position a single motif wherever you choose or work a row of small motifs as a border if you prefer.

Actual design measures:
1½ in (3.8 cm) square

Materials

Cotton and lace trimmed napkin
No 8 crewel needle
1 piece of 15-count waste canvas, measuring 2½ in (6.3 cm) square

Anchor stranded cottons (floss):

4 skeins of light blue (130)

2 skeins of dark blue (131)

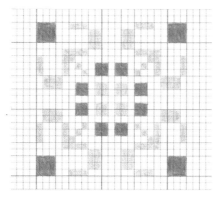

Instructions

Mark the centre of your square of waste canvas and tack (baste) it into position on your napkins. Using two strands of cotton (floss) and working over two strands of canvas in cross stitch throughout, stitch the design. When your embroidery is complete, remove the strands of waste canvas by pulling them from under your work with a pair of tweezers.

Delft Tablecloth

Look out at auctions and car boot (yard) sales for old cotton and lace tablecloths and, just by adding a motif here and there, working through waste canvas, you can transform and personalize your finds so they fit in with your room.

The cloth that I have used in this particular project measures 34 in (86.3 cm) square and is available as a kit (see stockists/suppliers information on page 165). Full details of the waste canvas technique are given on page 160.

Actual design measures:
large motif 3¼ in (8.25 cm) square; small motif approximately 1½ in (3.8 cm) square

Materials

1 panelled, lace and cotton tablecloth 34 in (86.3 cm) square (see stockists/suppliers information on page 165)
No 8 crewel needle
Contrasting sewing thread for tacking (basting)
8 pieces of 15-count waste canvas measuring 4 in (10 cm) square
8 pieces of 15-count waste canvas measuring 2½ in (6.3 cm) square
Pair of tweezers

Anchor stranded cottons (floss):

4 skeins of light blue (130)

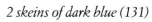

2 skeins of dark blue (131)

Instructions

Firstly mark the centre point of each of your squares of waste canvas. Using plain sewing thread tack (baste) your squares of waste canvas on to the plain cotton squares of your tablecloth, positioning them alternately, one large then one small, along the rows until all 16 plain squares of cloth are covered.

Using two strands of cotton (floss) and working in cross stitch throughout over two strands of canvas, start at the centre of your chart and work each motif in turn, taking care to ensure that all the patterning slopes in the same direction (you will notice that the squares lie at an angle on the cloth to form diamond images).

When you have completed your stitching, use tweezers to pull out the strands of waste canvas carefully from under your embroidery.

Delft Pot Holder

This clever little pot holder was bought ready-made, complete with Aida panel (see stockists/suppliers information on page 165). You can, however, make your own very easily and decorate it with a combination of tile motifs. For my pot holder I have used two large motifs side by side but, if preferred, you could use four small motifs, one at each corner, or a border of small motifs across the middle of the panel.

Actual design measures:
6½ × 3¼ in (16.5 × 8.25 cm)

Materials

1 piece of 14-count Aida in ecru measuring 7½ × 6½ in (19 × 16.5 cm).
No 7 crewel needle
2 pieces of towelling (terrycloth) measuring 8 in (20.5 cm) square
Sewing thread in a matching colour
1 piece of polyester wadding (synthetic batting) measuring 8 in (20 cm) square
1¾ yards (1.5 metres) of 1-in (2.5-cm) wide cotton ribbon to trim

Anchor stranded cottons (floss):

  1 skein of dark blue (131)
 1 skein of light blue (130)

Instructions

Find the centre of the Aida and the central point of the double tile chart and begin stitching here. Using three strands of cotton (floss) and cross stitch throughout, work the two large tiles side by side as indicated on the chart.

When your stitching is complete, set the Aida to one side and take the two squares of towelling (terrycloth), sandwiching the square of wadding (batting) in between.

My ready-made pot holder has been quilted with a sewing machine using diagonal lines of straight stitching. If you do not have a sewing machine simply sew the three layers of fabric together using a row of back stitch approximately ½ in (12 mm) from the edge of the fabric. You could quilt the fabric by hand if you are unable to find anything suitable that is ready-quilted.

Cut a length of ribbon measuring 7½ in (19 cm) long, fold this over the top edge of your worked Aida and sew it in place. Carefully lay your Aida right side up on top of your padded square of towelling, lining up the bottom edges. Tack (baste) into position along the side and bottom edges. Fold the remaining ribbon in half and, starting centre bottom, fold and pin it into position over your raw edges of fabric, leaving two loose ends at the centre top. Using back stitch, or better still a sewing machine, stitch the ribbon securely into position. Cross the loose tails at the top and join neatly to form a loop for hanging.

THE
STRAWBERRY
KITCHEN

Wild strawberries always remind me of holidays spent in the mountains of France so I have used this motif to accessorize a Provence-style kitchen. Summer fruits of all kinds are popular embroidery motifs and in traditional samplers a basket of fruit is said to symbolize fertility. In view of this, and just to be on the safe side, I have left out the baskets since the prospect of a band of pregnant cross-stitchers beating at my publisher's door is more than I can bear. Instead, I have used strawberry motifs of various styles and presented them within a mini sampler, complete with alphabet.

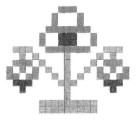

Strawberry Cushion Sampler

Using the waste canvas technique, this embroidery is cross stitched on to a ready-made cotton and lace cushion cover. Cushion covers of this style are easy to come by both through the major stores and in antique markets and auctions. When hunting out cottons and linens to embroider, try to select those incorporating plain fabric panels and let the shape of the panel suggest a design or the positioning of a design to you. Creating a sampler is always an interesting exploration of a motif since you can use a single image in many different ways, each of which may illustrate a mood or overall style for a piece of work. Experiment by working the same motif in different threads and on different backgrounds and then join your working samples together into a patchwork. Depending on size, this could then be transformed into a wall hanging or a book cover, or anything else that you feel might prove useful and attractive within your room.

Actual design measures:
4¾ × 5 in (12 × 12.7 cm)

Materials
*Cotton and lace cushion cover
 measuring 16 in (40.6 cm) square
 (see stockists/suppliers
 information on page 165)
Contrasting sewing thread for
 tacking (basting)
No 8 crewel needle
1 piece of 15-count waste canvas
 measuring 5½ in (14 cm) square
Pair of tweezers*

Anchor stranded cottons (floss):

 1 skein of pink (27)

 1 skein of rose (54)

 1 skein of green (265)

 1 skein of light pink (25)

Instructions
Mark the centre point of your waste canvas. Tack (baste) your waste canvas on to the central panel of your cushion cover with contrasting sewing thread.

Mark the centre of the chart and work from here, in cross stitch, using two strands of cotton (floss) and working over two strands of canvas. Please note that the design fits very snugly on to the central panel so be very careful to centre the work correctly. To double-check this, I suggest that you work the motif closest to the centre and then count outwards to the border so you can see exactly where it is positioned.

When you have completed the design, gently pull out the waste canvas threads from under the embroidery with the tweezers.

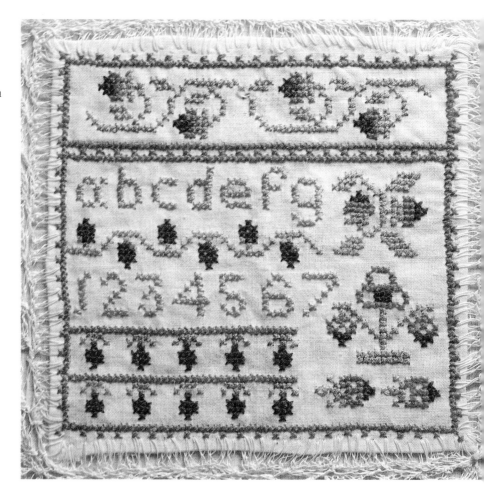

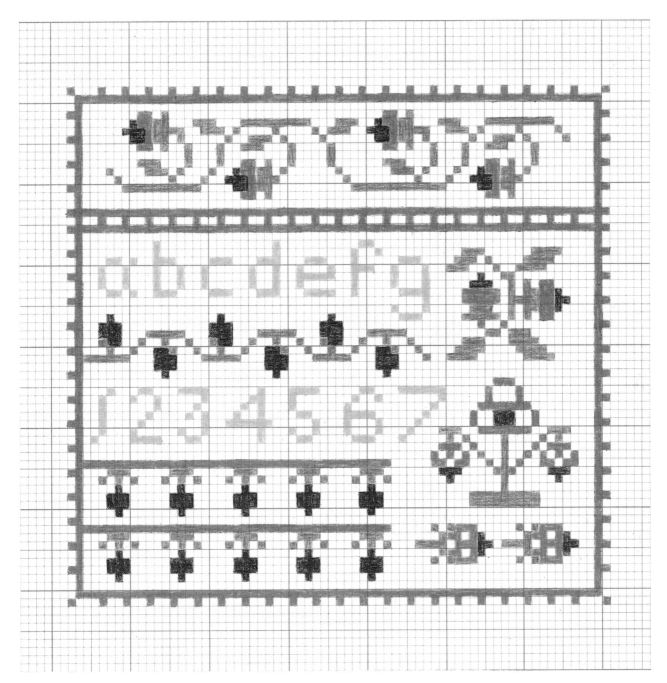

Below: Chart for waistband of Strawberry Apron

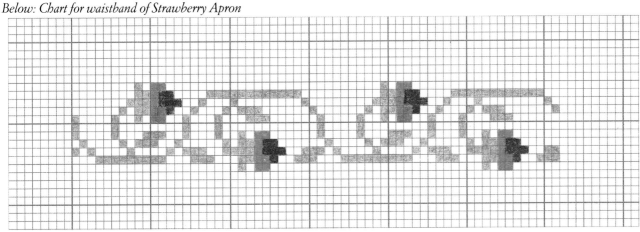

Strawberry Apron

For this project I have used the repeat motif at the top of the sampler to work a waistband for this pretty lace and cotton apron. I have also added interest by framing a single motif and using it as a patch on the pocket. The apron I used was bought ready-made and is available by mail order (see stockists/suppliers information on page 165). You can of course use the same chart for a waistband on a skirt or select a single motif and use it on the collar or pocket of a shirt. The waistband chart (see bottom of page 21) can be repeated to whatever length you wish and would also be useful as a trimming for a window blind (shade) or as a border for a plain cushion. If you have bench seating in your kitchen, why not make a long cushion to fit it and edge it with a strawberry border.

Actual designs measure:
waistband design area
13 × 1 in (33 × 2.5 cm);
pocket design area
2 × 1¾ in (5 × 4.5 cm)

Materials
Lace and cotton apron, available by
*   mail order (see stockists/suppliers*
*   information on page 165)*
No 8 crewel needle
1 strip of 15-count waste canvas to
*   fit the design area on the*
*   waistband plus 1 in (2.5 cm) extra*
*   – eg 14 × 2 in (35.5 × 5 cm)*
1 piece of 15-count waste canvas
*   measuring 3 in (7.5 cm) square*
Pair of tweezers

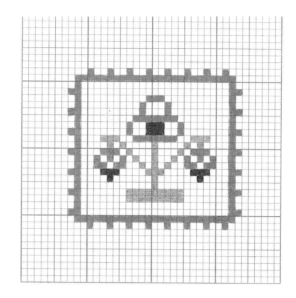

Anchor stranded cottons (floss):

 1 skein of pink (27)

 1 skein of rose (54)

1 skein of green (265)

Instructions
Tack (baste) the waste canvas into position, centring it on the waistband. Centre and tack the 3-in (7.5-cm) square of canvas to the pocket front.

Waistband Mark the centre of the waistband and the centre of the 62-stitch pattern repeat on the chart, ie stitch 31. Begin reading the chart from the centre, working in cross stitch with two strands of cotton (floss) over two strands of canvas. Work from the centre of the chart back to the left edge and then repeat the complete 62-stitch chart, reading it from right to left. Return to the centre, complete reading the second half of the chart from left to right, then repeat the whole 62-stitch chart, reading it from left to right. With tweezers, carefully pull out the strands of waste canvas from under the finished embroidery.

Pocket Mark the centre of the waste canvas on the pocket and the centre of the design on the chart. Work the entire motif in cross stitch using two strands of cotton over two strands of canvas. When the design is complete carefully pull out the strands of waste canvas from under the finished embroidery.

Strawberry Jam Pots

Home-made preserves taste delicious, look delicious and make very welcome gifts. These little jam pot lids are available complete with their own Aida panels, ready for you to add the embroidery. If you prefer you can make your own by cutting out a circle of Aida to the size of your jam pot lid and adding a lace trim around the edge.

Actual designs measure: 1¾ × 1½ in (4.5 × 3.8cm) and 1½ in (3.8 cm) square

Materials

2 ready-trimmed jam pot lids or two circles of 18-count Aida measuring approximately 3 in (7.5 cm) in diameter
1¼ yards (1 metre) of 2-in (5-cm) wide lace trim
No 8 crewel needle
Sewing thread to match the lace
Pencil

Anchor stranded cottons (floss):

 1 skein pink (27)
 1 skein rose (54)
 1 skein green (265)

Instructions

Mark the centre of the Aida band and the centre of your chart. If you are using ready-made lids simply work from the centre point in cross stitch using two threads of stranded cotton (floss). If you are making the pot lids for yourself, place the lid you intend to cover on the Aida and draw a circle in pencil around the neck. With sewing thread, oversew the edge in zigzag stitch to avoid fraying. Cut your length of lace in half and gather along one long edge, then stitch it carefully to the Aida circle.

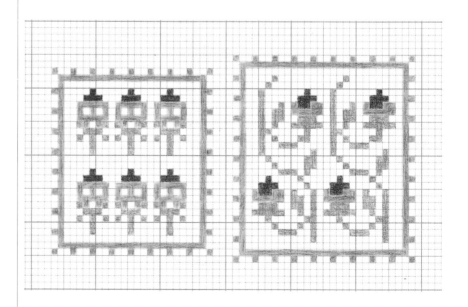

CHICKEN AND FISH STEW KITCHEN

I am lucky enough to occupy a design studio which overlooks a meadow and I have among my constant companions four very fat hens who free-range in front of my window. Through the other window there is a stream where, on a good day, one can find an exhausted salmon who has swum a very long way in order to get here. For this reason, I always associate country kitchens with chickens and fish and, since I am based in Wales, leeks are also a part of the picture.

A sampler is traditionally a practice piece made up in an assortment of stitches and illustrated with a number of different motifs. Why not select a collection of motifs that are personal to you and your family and incorporate them into your kitchen cross stitch work. Samplers are informal pieces and, to my mind, the designs on them should be placed at random surrounding one central panel. If you are design-shy, you can do as I have done and repeat the same motif to form a row, or work it as a series of mirror images.

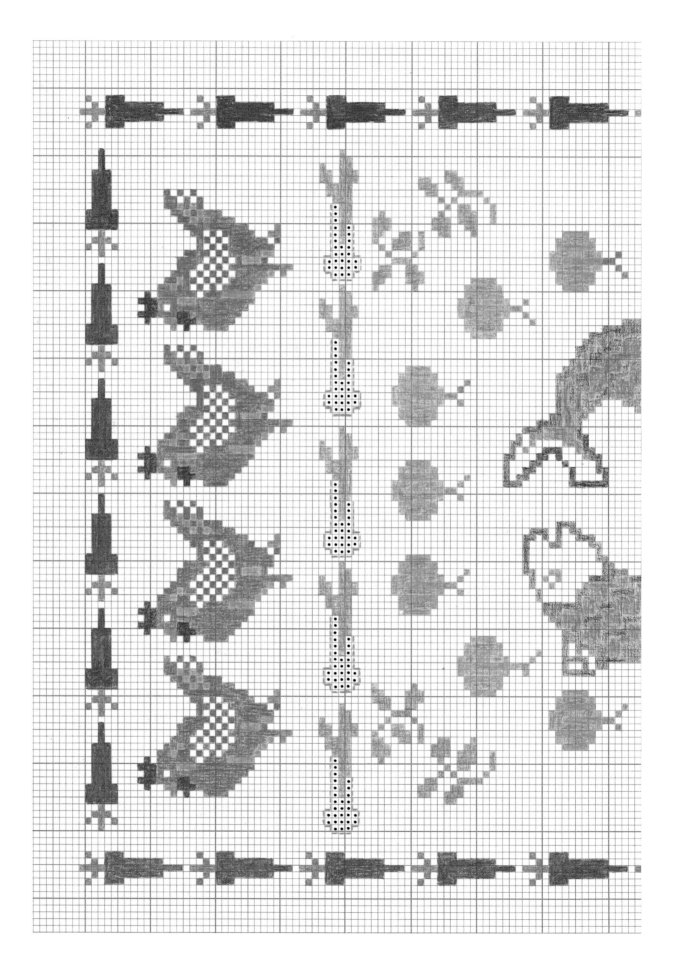

Chicken and Fish Stew Sampler

I have chosen to frame this piece and hang it on a wall, but it could also be used as the front cover for a binder or scrap book to keep your recipes in. You will find instructions for making up a folder in the Noah's Ark children's rooms section (see page 61).

Actual design measurements:
8¾ × 12½ in (22.25 × 31.75 cm)

Materials
1 piece of 14-count Aida measuring
   12 × 15 in (30.5 × 38 cm)
No 24 tapestry needle

The chart for the Chicken and Fish Stew Sampler is shown on pages 28–9.

Anchor stranded cottons (floss):

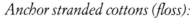
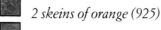

- 2 skeins of orange (925)
- 2 skeins of rust (326)
- 1 skein of caramel (362)
- 1 skein of orange (304)
- 1 skein of green (205)
- 1 skein of white (1)
- 1 skein of coral (10)
- 1 skein of khaki (903)
- 1 skein of red (335)

Instructions
Mark the centre of the chart and the centre of the Aida. Starting here, work in cross stitch using three strands of cotton (floss). When the design is complete, frame it according to your taste.

Fish Runner

Table runners are coming back into style and have never lost their popularity in mid-European countries. A Norwegian friend tells me that she has a complete set of embroidered table linens to cover every season so her kitchen welcomes in the spring with linens embroidered in greens and yellows, and provides a cosy setting for winter with red and green embroideries. She also has runners and napkins for special occasions such as Christmas and Easter, so she ensures her table always looks fresh and festive.

Actual design measures:
3½ × 4¾ in (8.9 × 12 cm)

Materials
No 8 crewel needle
Pins
Sewing thread for tacking (basting)
1 piece of 34-count ready-hemmed
   runner measuring 34½ × 8 in
   (86.8 × 20.5 cm)

Anchor stranded cottons (floss):

- 1 skein of coral (10)
- 2 skeins of khaki (903)
- 1 skein of green (205)

Instructions

Place a pin 2 in (5 cm) in from both sides and stitch a row of tacking (basting) from top to bottom at both ends. Place another pair of pins 2 in (5 cm) in from both the long edges of the runner and stitch two more rows of tacking top and bottom, the length of the runner. Find the centre right-hand edge of your chart and the centre of your right-hand vertical row of tacking and start here, working in cross stitch using two strands of cotton over two strands of linen. When the first block of fishes is complete, work the left-hand block of fishes, positioning them in the same way. Fold the runner in half horizontally and mark the centre. Mark the centre of your chart and begin the middle block of fishes here. Work in cross stitch throughout until the design is complete.

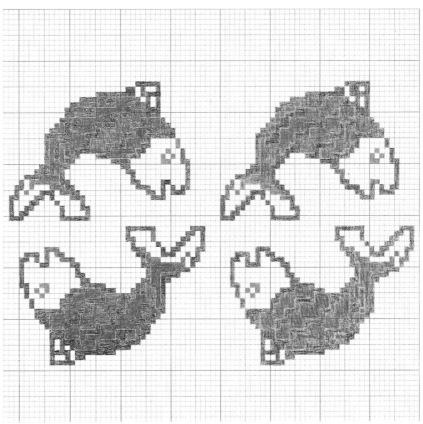

Chicken and Fish Salt Box

Squares of embroidered fabric can be used to decorate useful boxes of all kinds. Here I have used a whitewood salt box that I bought from a general store with the idea of keeping stock cubes in it – chicken for chicken, fish for fish, and so on. Work whichever panel suits your purpose.

Actual designs measure:
Chicken panel 3¼ × 2¾ in (8.25 × 7 cm)
Fish panel 3¾ × 2¾ in (9.5 × 7 cm)

Materials
1 piece of 14-count Aida measuring 6 in (15.25 cm) for each panel
1 piece of cardboard cut to fit each panel you intend covering
1 piece of polyester wadding (synthetic batting) the same size as the cardboard
No 24 tapestry needle
Rubber-based adhesive

FOR THE CHICKEN PANEL
Anchor stranded cottons (floss):

- *1 skein of green (205)*
- *1 skein of red (335)*
- *1 skein of caramel (362)*
- *1 skein of orange (304)*
- *1 skein of rust (326)*

FOR THE FISH PANEL
Anchor stranded cottons (floss):

- *1 skein of khaki (903)*
- *1 skein of green (205)*
- *1 skein of coral (10)*

Instructions
Mark the centre of the selected chart and the centre of the canvas. Starting here, work in cross stitch using three strands of cotton (floss) until the design is complete. Cut out the cardboard to fit the box front and glue the polyester wadding (synthetic batting) on top of the cardboard. Centre the panel of embroidery over the wadding and glue the edges to the back of the cardboard. Glue the mounted panels securely into position on the box and leave to dry.

Chicken Basket Liner

I have used an odd, scallop-edged napkin to make up this lining for a basket of eggs. You could choose to use a cheerful square of gingham or tartan fabric or simply hem the edges of a piece of sheeting for the same effect.

If you have drawn up your own motif and wish to increase its size, redraw it on square graph paper drawing four symbols for every one symbol on your original. When your design is complete you may want to round off the edges by rubbing out a few stitches here and there.

Actual design measures:
3 × 3½ in (7.5 × 8.9 cm)

Materials

1 white cotton napkin
1 piece of 15-count waste canvas
measuring 5 in (12.7 cm) square
No 8 crewel needle
Sewing thread for tacking (basting)
Pair of tweezers

Anchor stranded cottons (floss):

1 skein of rust (326)
1 skein of caramel (362)
1 skein of orange (304)
1 skein of red (335)

Instructions

Tack (baste) the waste canvas into position across one corner of the napkin. Mark the centre of the chart and the centre of the waste canvas and start here, working in cross stitch using two strands of cotton (floss) over two strands of canvas. Work until the design is complete. With tweezers, carefully remove the waste canvas from under the embroidery.

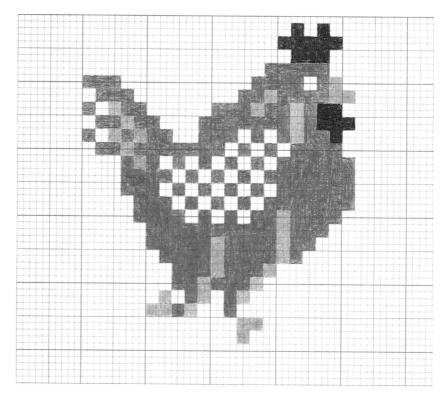

Nurseries

DUCKS, RABBITS AND MICE NURSERY

Baby animals of all sorts are popular friends in a baby's room and can be featured in numerous ways. Outlines from these cuddly characters can be traced and stencil-cut to create painted borders and motifs on walls, cupboards and cribs, or the single panels can be embroidered and framed as pictures in their own right. Use these motifs for birthday cards or embroider a row of ducks along the bottom of a little girl's dress – the possibilities are endless. Here are four ideas that I've come up with to get you started.

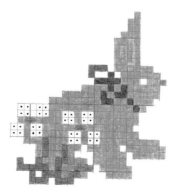

Ducks, Rabbits and Mice Patchwork Quilt

This pretty quilt can be made in no end of colour combinations. I have chosen to work the embroideries on pink Aida surrounded by traditional floral fabrics. You could achieve a fresh look by placing the embroideries among single coloured striped, spotted and gingham fabrics or, if you are a dab hand at quilting, you could quilt intricate panels on plain fabric and slot in the animals as and where you choose. Experiment with squared paper, drawing out a plan, and position the motifs in different ways. Produce more or less motif squares as you wish or work the designs on a white background and trim the quilt with broderie anglaise (eyelet lace). The following instructions are for the quilt you see in the photograph.

Actual designs measure: each square is 4 × 4½ in (10 × 11.5 cm)

Materials
6 pieces of 14-count pink Aida each measuring 6 in (15.25 cm) square
12 pieces of pale blue, 9 pieces of yellow and 8 pieces of pink lightweight cotton print fabric each measuring 6 in (15.25 cm) square
1 piece of cotton print for backing and border measuring 29½ × 40 in (75 × 101 cm)
1 piece of polyester wadding (synthetic batting) measuring 22 × 31 in (56 × 79 cm)
White sewing thread
No 8 crewel needle

TO MAKE 2 DUCK SQUARES
Anchor stranded cottons (floss):

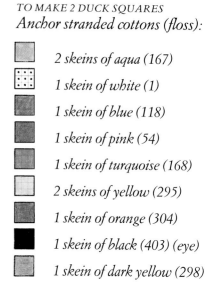

2 skeins of aqua (167)
1 skein of white (1)
1 skein of blue (118)
1 skein of pink (54)
1 skein of turquoise (168)
2 skeins of yellow (295)
1 skein of orange (304)
1 skein of black (403) (eye)
1 skein of dark yellow (298)

TO MAKE 2 MICE SQUARES
Anchor stranded cottons (floss):

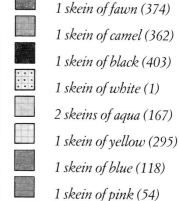

1 skein of fawn (374)
1 skein of camel (362)
1 skein of black (403)
1 skein of white (1)
2 skeins of aqua (167)
1 skein of yellow (295)
1 skein of blue (118)
1 skein of pink (54)
1 skein of mauve (109)

TO MAKE 2 RABBIT SQUARES
Anchor stranded cottons (floss):

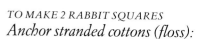
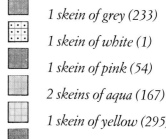

1 skein of grey (233)
1 skein of white (1)
1 skein of pink (54)
2 skeins of aqua (167)
1 skein of yellow (295)
.1 skein of blue (118)
1 skein of camel (362)
1 skein of green (266)

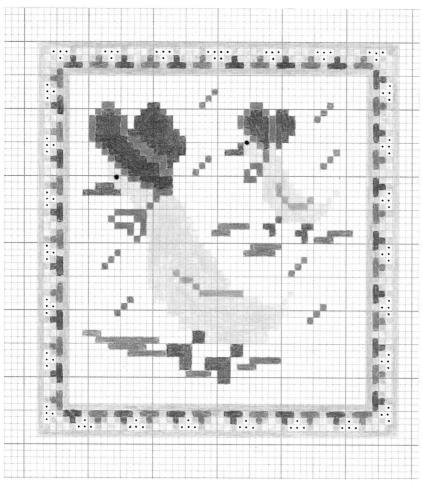

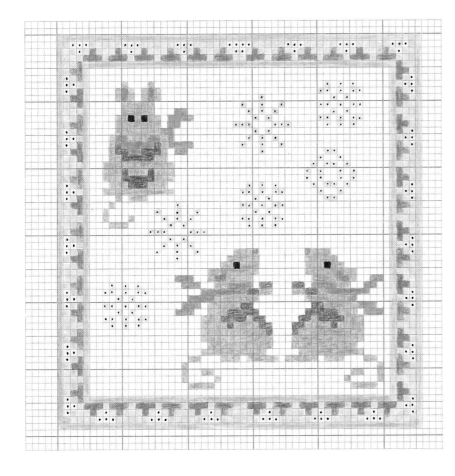

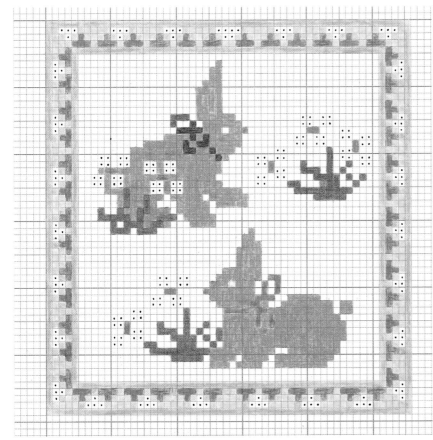

Instructions

Mark the centre of your charts and the centre of your Aida. Using three strands of cotton, work the designs in cross stitch starting here and following the charts. When the designs are complete, fold back the excess fabric and press, with a warm iron, laying the completed embroidery right side down over a towel. Take your cut squares of fabric and fold back and press the selvedges (selvages) so that all the squares are the same size. Pin together the squares in vertical strips, positioning them as the plan shows. Machine stitch or hand sew along the horizontal seams or individual square joins, taking care to line up the squares correctly. When you have completed the five strips of patches, join them vertically.

Lay out your backing fabric wrong side up. Lay the wadding (batting) on top and centre the patchwork, right side up, on top of the wadding. Turn the backing fabric over the wadding and tuck behind the patchwork edges. Pin the layers of fabric together and carefully machine stitch with a straight stitch around the edges of the patchwork top, so catching the backing into position. Hand finish the corners.

The plan for the Ducks, Rabbits and Mice Patchwork Quilt is shown on page 42.

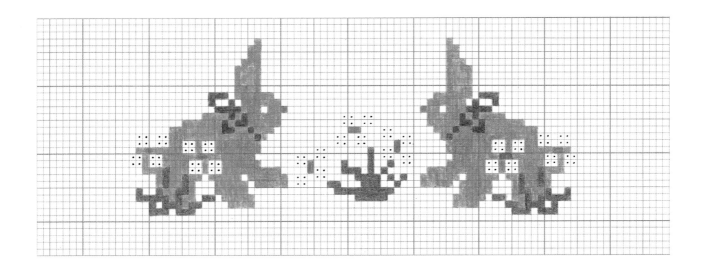

Rabbit Bib

Add these rabbits to a cheap towelling (terrycloth) bib to turn it into something special. You could also repeat this pattern to make a border of rabbits on a child's skirt or along a nursery blind (window shade) or curtain. Alter the colours of the rabbits and the flowers to add interest.

Actual design measures:
5 × 2 in (12.7 × 5 cm)

Materials

1 towelling (terrycloth) bib
1 piece of 14-count Aida measuring
* 7½ in (19 cm) – or 1 in (2.5 cm)*
* wider than the actual bib –*
* × 3 in (7.5 cm)*
2 lengths of ½-in (12-mm) wide
* satin ribbon, 1 in (2.5 cm) longer*
* than the actual bib*
No 8 crewel needle

Anchor stranded cottons (floss):

1 skein of grey (233)
1 skein of camel (362)
1 skein of blue (118)
1 skein of green (266)
1 skein of pink (54)
1 skein of white (1)

Instructions

Mark the centre of the chart and the centre of the Aida. Work in cross stitch from here, using three strands of cotton (floss). When the design is complete, turn under the short ends of the Aida and stitch into position across the bib. Pin lengths of ribbon along the top and bottom edges of the Aida. Hand sew or machine stitch in place.

Mice Nursery Bag

Taking a new baby out with you feels almost like moving house, there are so many bits of paraphernalia that have to travel with you, and how do you carry them? This smart bag could hold all your disposable nappies (diapers), feeds and toys and the handle allows you to hang it on your pushchair (stroller) without trailing it on the ground.

Actual design measures:
10¾ × 8¾ in (27.5 × 22.25 cm)

Materials

1 piece of 11-count Aida in ecru
   measuring 12½ in (31.25 cm)
   square
1 piece of heavyweight cotton tweed
   fabric measuring 20 × 44 in
   (51 × 111.75 cm)
1¼ yards (1 metre) of 1-in (2.5-cm)
   wide webbing for the handle
2 wooden toggles
1 spool of Kreinik Ombre Silver
   1000
No 8 crewel needle

Anchor stranded cottons (floss):

- 1 skein of fawn (374)
- 2 skeins of camel (362)
- 1 skein of yellow (295)
- 1 skein of blue (118)
- 1 skein of black (403)
- 1 skein of mauve (109)
- 3 skeins of aqua (167)
- 2 skeins of pink (54)
- 1 skein of white (1)
- 1 skein of aqua (167)
   plus Kreinik Silver
   (see above)

Instructions

Mark the centre of the chart and the centre of the canvas. Work in cross stitch from here using four strands of cotton (floss), with the exception of the snowflakes which are worked with one strand of silver thread and one strand of aqua (167) cotton. When the embroidery is complete, fold back the excess Aida and tack (baste), leaving a plain border measuring approximately ¾ in (19 mm).

Finishing

Lay out your cotton fabric and turn over the top and bottom (short ends) to form a hem 2½ in (6.3 cm) deep and hand sew or machine stitch in place. Fold the fabric in half, position the embroidered panel in the centre of the front half and neatly stitch into place around the edges. Fold the fabric in half with right sides facing and sew side seams. Turn right side out. Thread the webbing ends through the toggles and knot securely. Stitch the webbing to the top of the bag just above the toggles, positioning the ends over the side seams.

The chart for the Mice Nursery Bag is shown on pages 46–7.

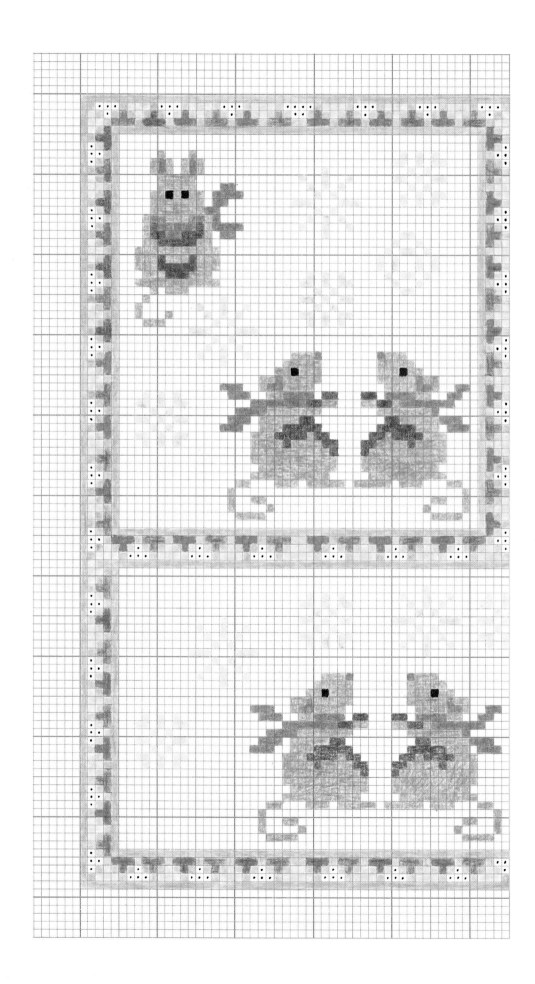

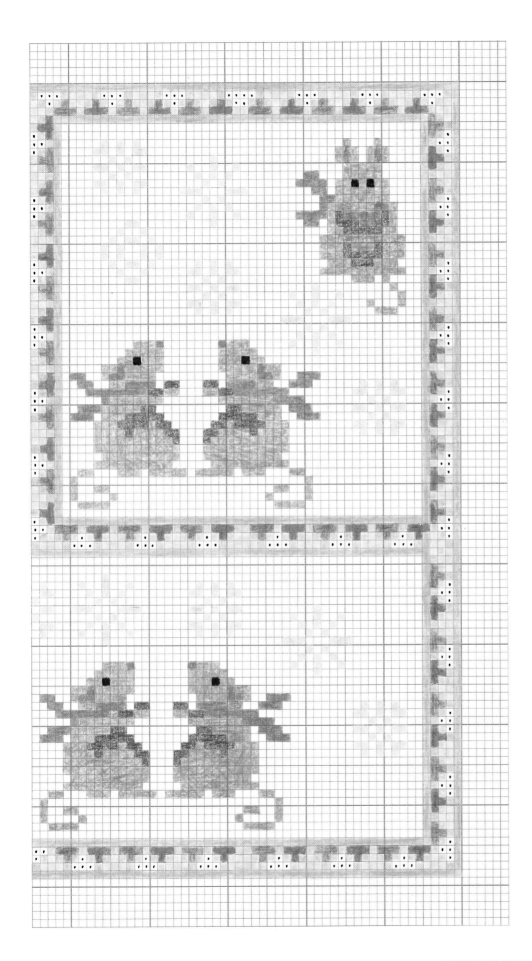

Duck Pillowcase Trim

Decorate a plain nursery pillowcase with ducks. You can repeat the baby ducks as many times as you wish or just work the mother duck on her own. If you wish, you could repeat the border right around the pillowcase – it all depends on how much work you feel like putting into the project. Or why not work the ducks as a yoke across a baby's dress? This design is worked using the waste canvas method, full details of which can be found on page 160.

Actual design (ducks only) measures:
7 × 3 in (17.8 × 7.5 cm)

Materials

Cotton pillowcase trimmed with broderie anglaise (eyelet lace), measuring approximately 17½ × 13 in (44.5 × 33 cm)
1 piece of 15-count waste canvas measuring 6 in (15.25 cm) long × the width of the pillowcase
Contrasting sewing thread for tacking (basting)
No 7 crewel needle
Pair of tweezers

Anchor stranded cottons (floss):

1 skein of aqua (167)
1 skein of white (1)
1 skein of blue (118)
1 skein of pink (54)
1 skein of turquoise (168)
1 skein of yellow (295)
1 skein of orange (304)
1 skein of black (403) (eye)
1 skein of dark yellow (298)

Instructions

Tack (baste) the waste canvas into the desired position on the pillowcase. Work the bottom border first, using two strands of cotton (floss) in cross stitch throughout. Work the ducks, starting with the mother and adding as many little ones as you wish. Work them in cross stitch with the exception of the eyes, which are worked as small black straight stitches. When the ducks are complete, work the top border. When the embroidery is complete, carefully remove the waste canvas from under your stitches with tweezers.

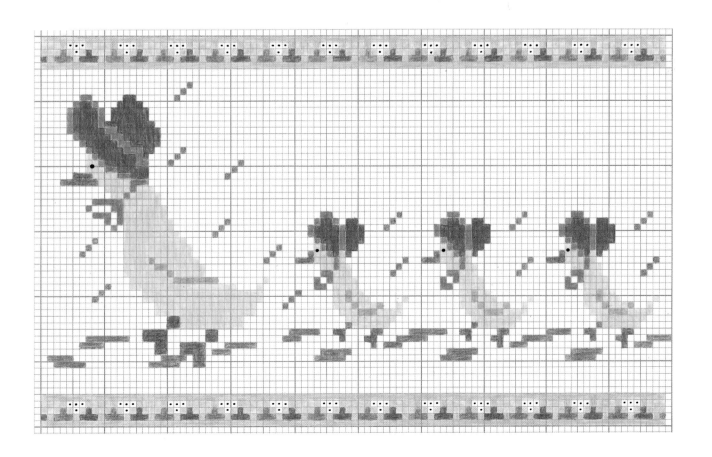

CLOWNS, STARS AND NUMBERS PLAYROOM

Clowns and stars in primary colours will brighten up a child's playroom and be popular with both boys and girls. Add some numbers or letters and learning will become a matter of fun.

Clowns can be used in lots of ways. You can stitch them on Binca, cut them to shape and back them in felt to make cuddly soft toys. Frame them individually, stitch them on paper to use as a mobile or even cross stitch one on a sweatshirt.

For very young kids, why not make your own set of bricks using the stars and numbers charts. Work six equally-sized squares of Binca, using a different number or star on each one, and stitch them together over a foam block to form a soft, washable brick. Here are some other ideas for you.

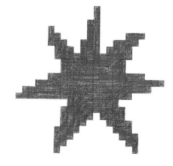

Clown Bag

This jolly bag is very easy to make and could be used for laundry, shoes, toys or anything else that is best hidden away in a bag. I have used a simple drawstring opening, but you could cut the front panel 8 in (20.5 cm) shorter than the back panel and fold over the back panel to form a flap which could be fastened to the front with toggles. Add two straps to the back and you have a rucksack (backpack) or school bag. The following instructions are to make the bag that has been photographed.

Actual design measures:
15 × 5 in (38 × 12.7 cm)

Materials

1 piece of 11-count Aida measuring
    18 × 7 in (45.7 × 17.8 cm)
2 pieces of heavyweight cotton fabric
    each measuring 20 × 30 in
    (50.8 × 76.2 cm)
2¾ yards (2½ metres) of white cord
Sewing thread to match the backing
No 23 tapestry needle
2 beads

Anchor stranded cottons (floss):

- *1 skein of yellow (298)*
- *1 skein of turquoise (410)*
- *1 skein of mauve (99)*
- *1 skein of orange (304)*
- *1 skein of red (335)*
- *1 skein of black (403)*
- *1 skein of green (227)*
- *1 skein of flesh (893)*

Instructions

Mark the centre of the chart and the centre of the Aida. Starting here, work in cross stitch using four strands of cotton (floss). When the design is complete, take one piece of heavyweight cotton fabric and centre your panel across the bottom approximately 1½ in (3.8 cm) from the bottom and side edges after allowing approximately ¾ in (19 mm) of the cotton for turning under. Machine seam or back stitch into position, turning under approximately ¾ in (19 mm) of the canvas at the edges. When the embroidery is stitched into position, turn back the top of the red fabric to create a hem, 2 in (5 cm) deep, through which to thread your cord. Take the second piece of cotton fabric and hem the top to match. Place the two pieces of fabric together face to face and machine or back stitch the side and bottom seams. Turn right side out. Cut the length of cord in half and thread one piece through the top back hem and one piece through the top front hem. Thread the two double ends of cord through one bead each and knot to secure.

Juggling Stars

Everybody is juggling. It is therapeutic, relaxing and helps to improve your co-ordination. Make these juggling balls with scraps of fabric and decorate them with cross stitch stars or numbers. Stuff them with lentils or dried beans.

Actual design measures: approximately 2 in (5 cm) square

Materials
3 pieces of 11-count Aida measuring 4 in (10 cm) square
1 piece of silver lurex or felt measuring 31½ × 6 in (80 × 15.25 cm)
14 oz (400 g) lentils or dried beans
Sewing thread to match fabric
No 23 tapestry needle

Anchor stranded cottons (floss):

1 skein of red (335)

1 skein of turquoise (410)

1 skein of green (227)

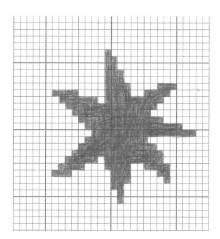

Instructions
Mark the centre of the charts and the centre of the Aida. Starting here, work in cross stitch using four strands of cotton (floss) until you have completed the three star panels. Take your silver fabric or felt and cut out six circles

approximately 4½ in (11.5 cm) in diameter (use a jar top as a template). Centre the squares of embroidered Aida on three of the circles of fabric and back stitch into position, turning under the edges of the Aida so the finished panels are approximately 2½ in (6.3 cm)

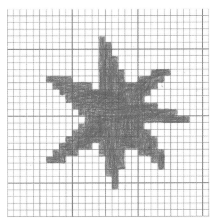

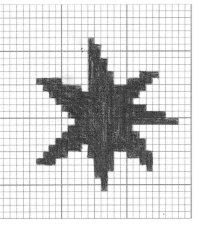

square. Take the three remaining circles of fabric and place them right sides together over the embroidered circles. Stitch firmly around the edges leaving a 2 in (5 cm) gap. Turn the circles right side out and fill with the lentils or dried beans. Firmly stitch up the remaining gaps.

Clown Card

Children love receiving personalized greetings cards. You can insert the correct age using the number chart, so could adapt this design for other significant birthdays for adults.

Actual design measures:
4½ in (11.5 cm) square

Materials
1 piece of 14-count Aida measuring
  6 × 7 in (15.25 × 17.8 cm)
1 piece of cardboard measuring
  17½ × 8¼ in (43.5 × 21 cm)
No 24 tapestry needle
Craft knife
Rubber-based adhesive

Anchor stranded cottons (floss):

1 skein of yellow (298)
1 skein of turquoise (410)
1 skein of mauve (99)
1 skein of red (335)
1 skein of green (227)
1 skein of flesh (893)
1 skein of black (403)

Instructions
Mark the centre of the chart and the centre of the Aida. Starting here, work the design in cross stitch using three strands of cotton (floss). Take your card and fold it into three equal parts horizontally. Cut a rectangle in the centre panel to fit the design. Glue the finished embroidery on to the centre of the left-hand panel. Apply glue to the surround of the cut-out area on the centre panel, tuck the embroidered panel in and press down.

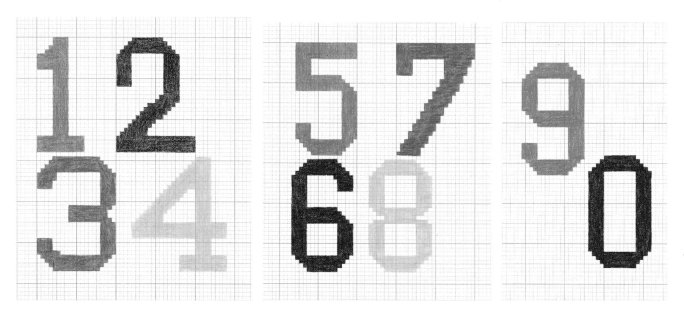

Clown Grow Chart

Use this fun chart to keep track of how the children are growing. The sliding flags will help you to identify who has reached which height and will save you having to make marks on your walls.

Materials

1 piece of 14-count Aida measuring 43 × 6½ in (109.25 × 16.5 cm)
1 piece of white sheeting measuring 43 × 6½ in (109.25 × 16.5 cm)
1 length of 1-in (2.5-cm) wide ribbon measuring 62 in (157.5 cm) long
White sewing thread
No 25 tapestry needle
A tape measure
3 heavy beads or weights
8-in (20.5-cm) batten or stick for hanging
Rubber-based adhesive
Coloured cardboard

Anchor stranded cottons (floss):

- *1 skein of yellow (298)*
- *2 skeins of turquoise (410)*
- *2 skeins of mauve (99)*
- *1 skein of red (335)*
- *1 skein of black (403)*
- *1 skein of green (227)*
- *1 skein of flesh (893)*
- *1 skein of orange (304)*

Instructions

Allowing ½ in (12 mm) waste at each edge, count up from the bottom to find the position of the first turquoise star. Starting here, begin following the chart in cross stitch, using two strands of cotton (floss) throughout. Work the straight stitch detail in black, using two strands of cotton.

Finishing

Lay the completed design on top of the strip of sheeting and turn in and pin ½ in (12 mm) of waste on all edges. Stitch the edges, preferably with a sewing machine or by back stitching, leaving a 1-in (2.5-cm) gap at the top of both side seams for your hanging stick. Take your ribbon and make a loop at the top for your stick. Cut the bottom so that the ribbon is the same length as your chart. Take your tape measure and cut off the bottom portion so that it begins at 19½ in (49.5 cm). Glue this to the length of your ribbon. Make flags with your children's names by cutting circles from the cardboard and making two horizontal slits, approximately 1 in (2.5 cm) apart and 1 in (2.5 cm) wide in each one. Write your child's name above the top slit. Slide these flags on to your ribbon. Loop the tape measure over the stick to hang beside your completed grow chart. Tie one bead or weight at each bottom corner of the chart and one at the bottom of the tape.

NOAH'S ARK CHILDREN'S ROOM

Do you remember starting school and wanting your very own desk to study on at home? This group of designs is especially for kids who are beginning to take an interest in their surroundings and treasuring all those things that make school times interesting. The story is an old one . . . Mr and Mrs Noah and their followers saving the world with their Ark. You can mix and match the animals as you choose (provided you keep them in twos) or you could use different motifs that reflect the child's hobbies or interests or encourage them to produce cross stitch panels of their own which you could make into interesting schooltime accessories. The possibilities are endless.

Ark Folder

If you have some leftover curtain material or even wallpaper, you could make up this folder which can be used as a scrapbook, a collector's album or simply a project folder. I have used cotton ticking but any medium-weight fabric would do.

Actual design measures:
13¼ × 9 in (33.6 × 22.9 cm)

Materials

1 piece of 11-count Aida measuring
  12 × 17 in (30.5 × 43 cm)
2 pieces of cotton ticking each
  measuring 17 × 22 in
  (43 × 56 cm)
2 pieces of red felt each measuring
  12 × 17 in (30.5 × 43 cm)
2¼ yards (2 metres) wool (yarn),
  ribbon or tape for ties
1¼ yards (1 metre) ½-in (12-mm)
  wide ribbon to hold paper
2 pieces of stiff cardboard each
  measuring 13½ × 18½ in
  (34.25 × 47 cm)
Sheet of paper measuring
  11½ × 16½ in (29 × 42 cm)
Rubber-based adhesive
White sewing thread
No 8 crewel needle
Hole punch
Pencil

Anchor stranded cottons (floss):

- *1 skein of black (403)*
- *1 skein of grey (233)*
- *1 skein of fawn (362)*
- *1 skein of yellow (291)*
- *2 skeins of blue (131)*
- *1 skein of aqua (168)*
- *1 skein of red (334)*
- *1 skein of brown (936)*
- *1 skein of flesh (868)*
- *1 skein of turquoise (410)*
- *1 skein of lime (279)*
- *1 skein of green (256)*
- *1 skein of pink (894)*
- *·1 skein of white (1)*
- *1 skein of greenish blue (203)*

Instructions

Mark the centre of the chart and the centre of the Aida, and work from here in cross stitch using three strands of cotton (floss) and adding the final straight stitch detail in colours as indicated on the key by the chart.

Cover the back of one piece of cardboard in ticking, folding the waste to the inside and glue down. Using the made-up back cover as a guide, pin the sampler to the centre of the remaining piece of ticking, folding under the edges so you have a plain ½ in (12 mm) border of Aida all around your picture. Stitch this into position over the ticking and use it to cover the remaining piece of board.

Using odd pieces of wool (yarn), make four twisted cords 11 in (28 cm) long. Glue two of these to the inside of the back cover 6 in (15.25 cm) from top and bottom, and two to the inside of the front cover, 5 in (12.7 cm) from top and bottom. Glue the red felt to the inside of both covers.

Take your paper and with the hole punch make two holes at the left side edge. Place these inside the back of your folder and mark the positions of the two holes with a pencil. Glue the centre of your length of ribbon to the inside back cover between and over the position of the punched holes, leaving the ends free (see diagram). Glue a piece of stiff card over the ribbon to secure it in place. Thread ribbons through the holes in your paper and tie in a bow.

The chart for the Ark Folder is shown on pages 62–3.

Inside back
Glue card over ribbon to secure

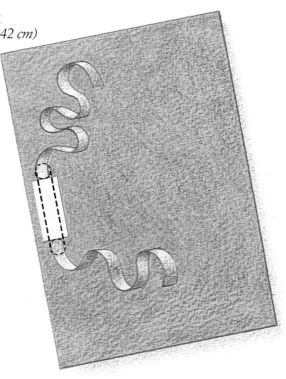

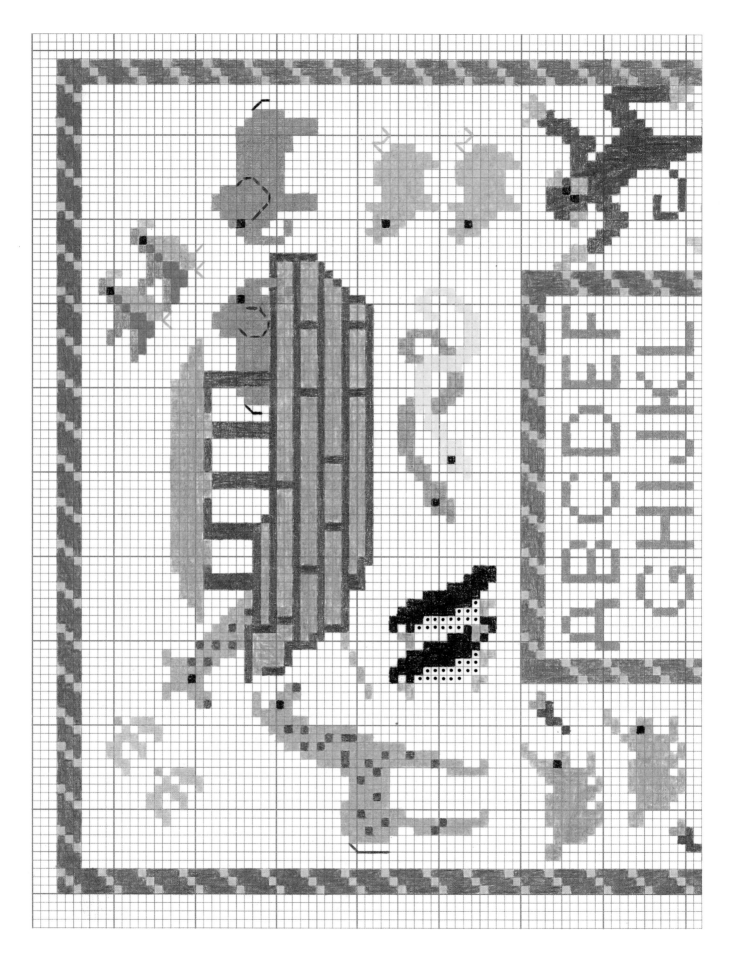

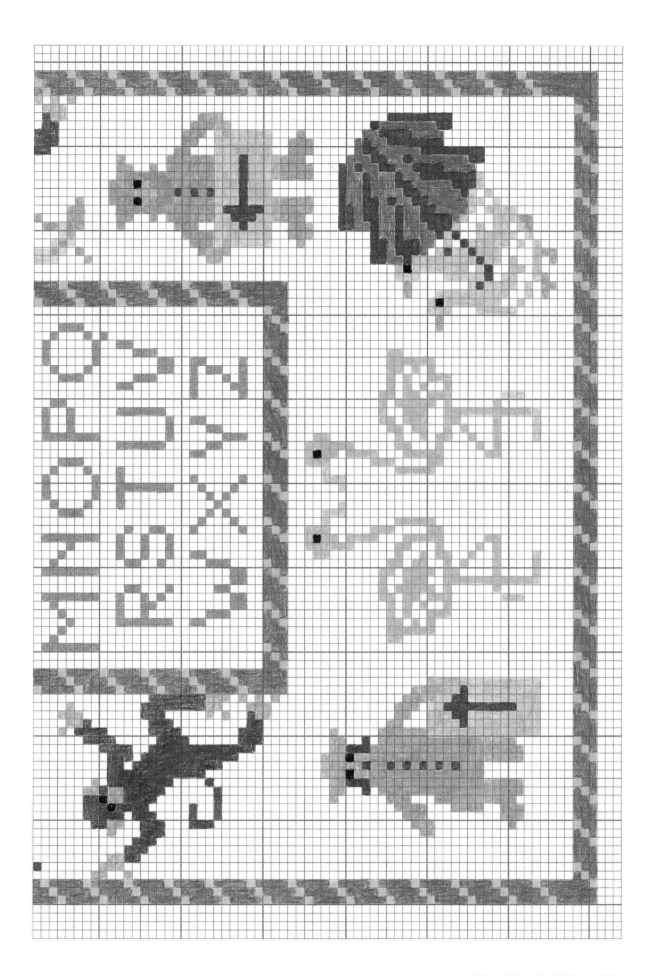

Ark Door Plate

This panel of cross stitch can be used as a door plate, if protected with a suitable piece of perspex, or you could add a fringe and use it as a bookmark. Why not leave out the lovebirds and embroider your child's name instead, or choose your favourite animals to fill the panels?

Actual design measures:
9½ × 2⅓ in (24 × 5.9 cm)

Materials
1 piece of 14-count Aida measuring 11½ × 3 in (29.2 × 7.5 cm)
1 perspex door plate (see stockists/ suppliers information on page 165)
No 8 crewel needle
Cardboard
Glue

Anchor stranded cottons (floss):

- 1 skein of grey (233)
- 1 skein of yellow (291)
- 1 skein of blue (131)
- 1 skein of aqua (168)
- 1 skein of pale green (203)
- 1 skein of brown (936)
- 1 skein of flesh (868)
- 1 skein of turquoise (410)
- 1 skein of black (403)
- 1 skein of red (334)
- 1 skein of green (256)

Instructions
Mark the centre of the chart and the centre of the Aida and, using three strands of cotton (floss), work in cross stitch from here. Add details in straight stitch as indicated on the chart. When the embroidery is complete, mount it on a piece of cardboard the same size as the door plate by folding the waste fabric to the back and glueing it down or following the manufacturer's instructions.

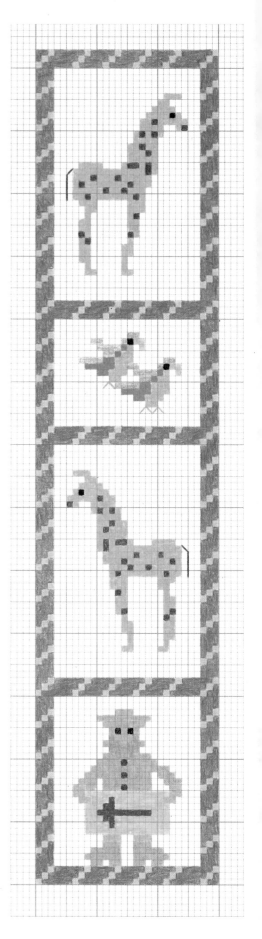

Ark Pencil Holder

This handy pencil holder can be kept hanging on the wall or can be folded and used as a pencil case. I have used the same ticking for all these projects, but you could of course use a co-ordinating plain coloured fabric if you preferred.

Actual design measures:
11½ in × 4½ in (29.2 × 11.5 cm)

Materials

1 piece of 14-count Aida measuring 13½ × 6½ in (34.3 × 16.5 cm)
1 piece of cotton ticking or medium-weight fabric measuring 22 × 14 in (55.8 × 35.5 cm)
Sewing thread to match fabric
No 8 crewel needle
Two small squares of self-adhesive Velcro

Anchor stranded cottons (floss):

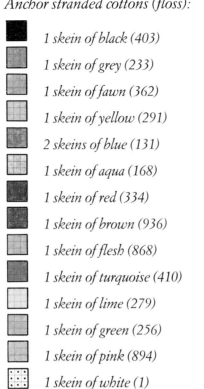

1 skein of black (403)
1 skein of grey (233)
1 skein of fawn (362)
1 skein of yellow (291)
2 skeins of blue (131)
1 skein of aqua (168)
1 skein of red (334)
1 skein of brown (936)
1 skein of flesh (868)
1 skein of turquoise (410)
1 skein of lime (279)
1 skein of green (256)
1 skein of pink (894)
1 skein of white (1)
1 skein of greenish blue (203)

Instructions

Mark the centre of the chart and the centre of the Aida. Using three strands of cotton (floss), work from here in cross stitch, adding detail in straight stitch as indicated on the chart. When the embroidery is complete set it aside.

Turn back the ticking by ½ in (12 mm) on all sides and hem in place. Fold up the bottom edge to make the pocket, approximately 6½ in (16.5 cm) deep, and stitch the side seams. Pin the embroidery to the centre of the pocket, folding back the waste Aida after leaving a border of approximately ½ in (12 mm) all around the finished embroidery. Stitch the side and bottom edges of this panel to the ticking.

Tack (baste) the top of the Aida panel to the ticking pocket to form three separate channels for pencils, pens, etc. Make a 2-in (5-cm) hem at the top of the ticking to hold a ruler. Stick two pieces of Velcro at the back of the pencil holder with corresponding pieces stuck to the chosen position on the wall.

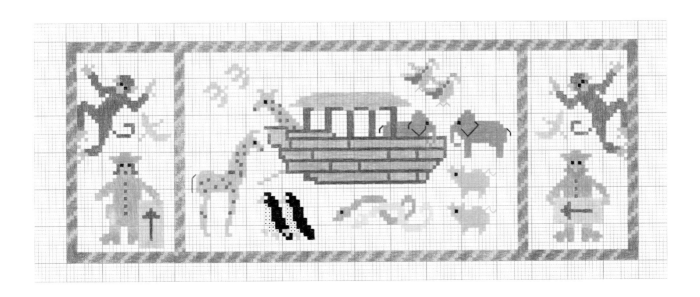

Ark Window Blind (Shade)

It is easy to make a fabric window blind (shade) or stitch a border on to an existing one. Blinds can be bought ready-made, in plain colours, very cheaply. Alternatively, you could use this border design as a frieze along the edge of a shelf or on the pelmet (valance) of a curtain.

Actual design measures:
21 × 2½ in (53.3 × 6.3 cm)

Materials

1 piece of 11-count Aida measuring the width of your window – minimum 26 × 5¾ in (66 × 14.6 cm) – × the length
1 piece of cotton ticking or heavyweight cotton measuring the width of your window (with the same minimum as above) × the length plus 5 in (12.7 cm)
No 8 crewel needle
Wooden batten (hanging rod) slightly wider than the blind
Small length of cord in a toning colour
1 bead

Anchor stranded cottons (floss):

- ■ *1 skein of black (403)*
- ▨ *1 skein of grey (233)*
- ▥ *1 skein of fawn (362)*
- ▥ *1 skein of yellow (291)*
- ▥ *1 skein of aqua (168)*
- ▩ *1 skein of red (334)*
- ▨ *1 skein of brown (936)*
- ▥ *1 skein of flesh (868)*
- ▨ *1 skein of turquoise (410)*
- ▢ *1 skein of lime (279)*
- ▥ *1 skein of green (256)*
- ▥ *1 skein of pink (894)*
- ⚅ *1 skein of white (1)*
- ▥ *1 skein of greenish blue (203)*

Instructions

Mark the centre of the chart and the centre of the Aida. Start here, using four strands of cotton (floss) to work the design in cross stitch. Add straight stitch detail as indicated on the chart. When the embroidery is complete set it aside.

Turn back and hem the long edges of your ticking to the required width. Turn over and stitch the top of the ticking, leaving a hem wide enough to take a wooden rod – approximately 1 in (2.5 cm) wide. Hem the bottom of the ticking about 2 in (5 cm) from the bottom. Stitch it carefully to the blind (shade) using back stitch, or machine stitch it. Thread a length of cord through the bottom centre of the blind. Thread on the bead and tie a knot in the cord to hold the bead in place.

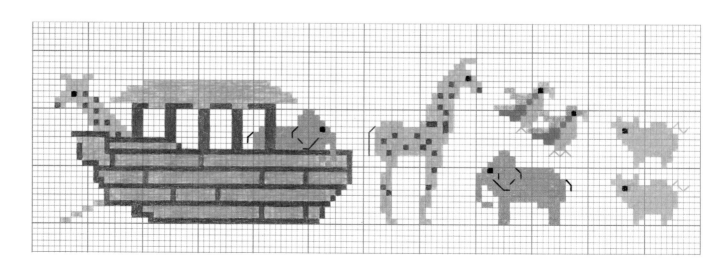

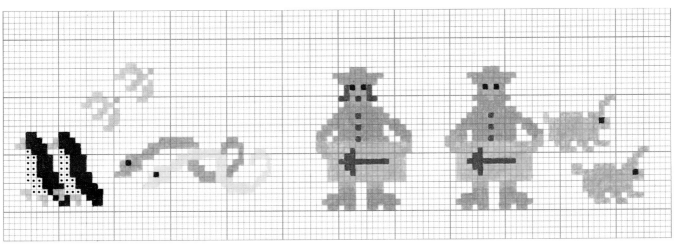

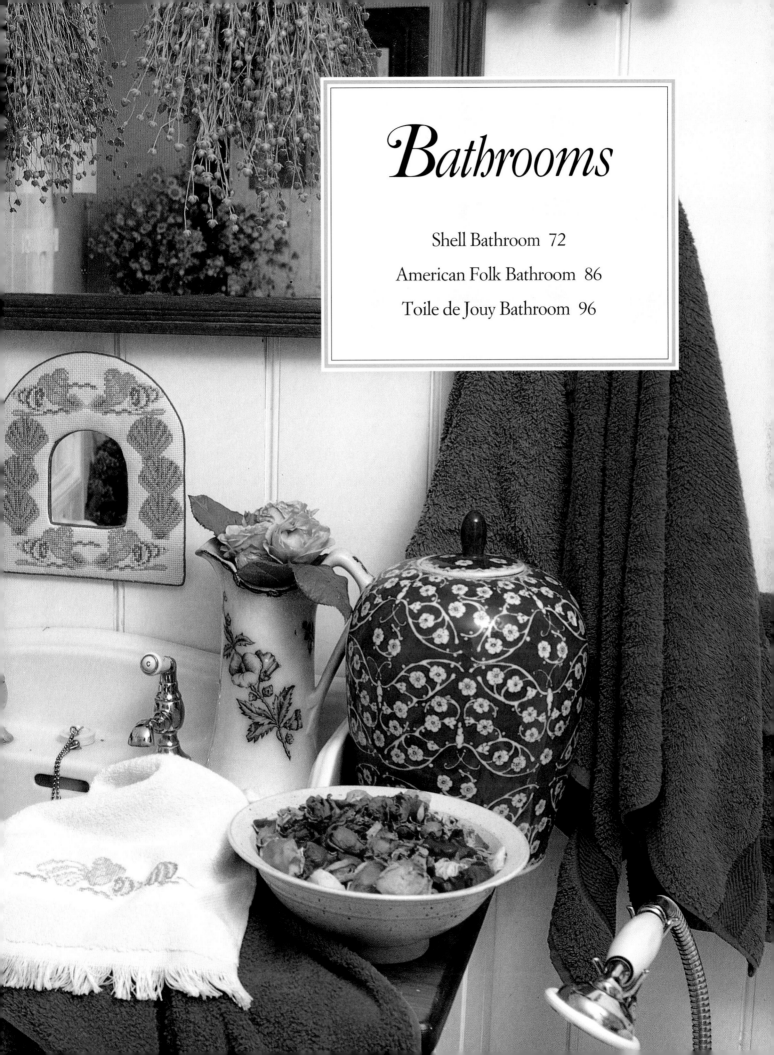

Bathrooms

SHELL
BATHROOM

Seashells, with their pretty pearly colours and interesting shapes, are a popular source of inspiration to both the embroiderer and the interior designer. Wallpapers, fabrics, friezes and stencils can be used in contrast or harmony to create a theme for a bathroom, and real shells displayed in flat baskets or glass bottles will add an extra decorative dimension.

For the following projects I have selected and emphasized the soft pinks and creams one associates with shells and drawn abstract shell shapes which will fit in with a modern interior. You might prefer a more delicate approach, in which case you could work these charts on a finer canvas or linen and use a palette of creams and golds for your embroidery. You might choose to follow a colour scheme already dictated by a wall-paper or tile, but the important thing is to use your embroidery skills to accessorize your room with complementary images.

Shell Mirror Frame

I couldn't resist using a mirror image on this mirror frame design. You could add extra interest by incorporating some glittery thread or glueing real shells around the edge or on top of the design to make it three-dimensional. Pretty mirror frames have the advantage of improving the way you feel about yourself – especially first thing in the morning.

Actual design measures:
8¾ × 9 in (22.25 × 22.9 cm)

Materials

1 piece of 11-count Aida measuring 12 in (30.5 cm) square
2 pieces of mounting card (mat board) each measuring 9¼ × 8½ in (23.4 × 21.6 cm)
1 piece of polyester wadding (synthetic batting) measuring 9¼ × 8½ in (23.4 × 21.6 cm)
1 sheet of paper measuring 10 × 9½ in (25.4 × 24 cm)
Pencil
Rubber-based adhesive
1¾ yards (1.5 metres) of coloured cord for edging
1 mirror tile measuring a minimum of 4½ in (11.5 cm) square
No 24 tapestry needle
Scalpel or craft knife

Anchor stranded cottons (floss):

2 skeins of rose (894)
2 skeins of pink (868)
1 skein of silver (234)
1 skein of turquoise (168)
1 skein of light turquoise (167)
1 skein of gold (362)
1 skein of yellow (295)
1 skein of dark grey (233)
1 skein of white (1)

Instructions

Mark the centre of your Aida and the centre of your chart and count onwards from here to find a starting point for your design. Work the design entirely in cross stitch using three strands of cotton (floss) throughout.

Fold the paper in half vertically. Draw half an arched window shape against the centre fold, using the template as a guide. Trace this shape on to both sheets of mounting card (mat board) and cut them out. Cut the centre window in the same way from one piece of board only. Cut the polyester wadding (synthetic batting) to the same shape and glue into place on top of the piece of mounting card with the cut-out window.

Take your finished embroidery and carefully glue it to the board, stretching it over the cut-out window and glueing it at the back of the board. With a craft knife, cut out the centre of the canvas leaving about ½ in (12 mm) for turning back. Slit, turn back and glue this remaining canvas using the template as a guide. Glue the mirror to the centre of the back board, positioning it to correspond with the front opening. Glue the boards together. Carefully glue the cord around the edge of the mirror and the outer edge of the embroidery.

The chart for the Shell Mirror Frame is shown on pages 76–7.

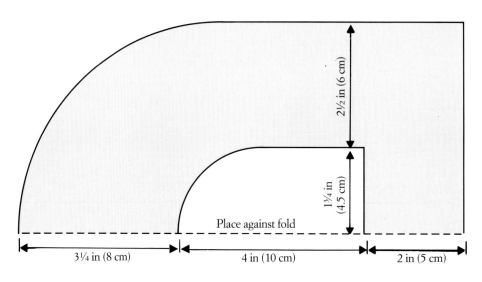

2½ in (6 cm)

1¾ in (4.5 cm)

Place against fold

3¼ in (8 cm) 4 in (10 cm) 2 in (5 cm)

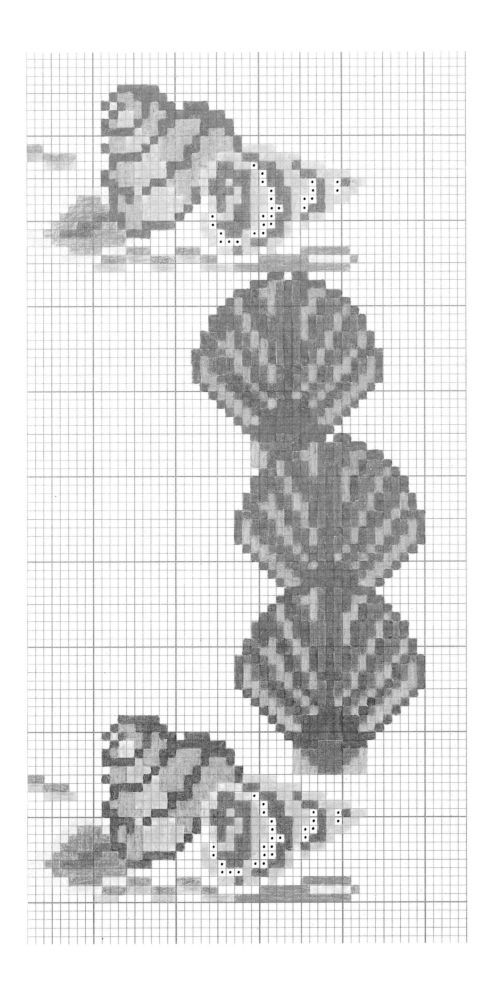

Shell Guest Towel

Many embroidery shops and department stores now sell towels with Aida borders ready for cross stitching. If you have a plain towel that you want to use, simply cut a strip of Aida measuring approximately ½ in (12 mm) more than your required width and depth, work your design on it and then fold back the waste canvas and hand sew or machine stitch it into position on your towel. If you do not want to create a border design you can produce individual motifs on squares of canvas and stitch them to the towel in the same way. Use an initial to personalize a very special gift.

Actual design measures:
6¾ × 2¾ in (17.1 × 7 cm)

Materials
1 guest towel with a strip of
*   14-count Aida, or a strip of Aida*
*   to fit it*
No 24 tapestry needle

Anchor stranded cottons (floss):

1 skein of steel grey (233)
1 skein of grey (231)
1 skein of tan (374)
1 skein of white (1)
1 skein of gold (362)
1 skein of light turquoise (167)
1 skein of turquoise (168)
1 skein of pink (868)
1 skein of rose (894)
1 skein of silver (234)

Instructions
Mark the centre of your chart and the centre of the Aida. Start here, working the design entirely in cross stitch using three strands of cotton (floss).

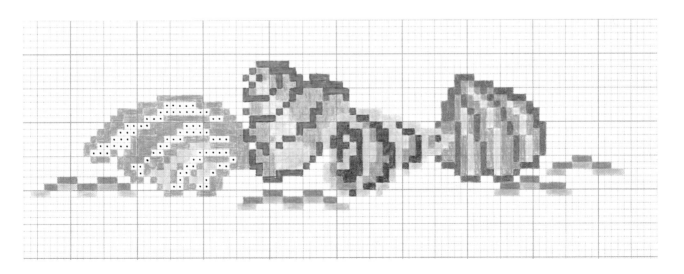

Shell Make-up Bag

This make-up or bathroom accessory bag can either be hung on the wall or folded up and taken on your travels. I have used a standard-sized guest towel and embroidered a Binca panel in soft cottons (floss). The real shells are added at the end to complete the picture.

Materials

Peach hand towel measuring
*   *18 × 33 in (45.7 × 83.8 cm)*
1 piece of 6-count Binca measuring
*   *15 × 12 in (38 × 30.5 cm)*
1 reel (spool) of Kreinik gold cord
Sewing thread
No 23 tapestry needle
10 shells
Glue
Crochet hook

Anchor Coton à Broder:

1 skein of grey (398)
1 skein of butter (386)
1 skein of donkey (667)
1 skein of aqua (168)
1 skein of slate (235)
1 skein of rose (895)
1 skein of pink (892)
1 skein of silver (397)

Instructions

Mark the centre of the chart and the centre of the canvas. Start here, working the design in cross stitch using one strand of all colours except pink (892), which should be used together with one strand of gold cord. Work the main body of the design in cross stitch and use star stitch (see the diagrams below) as indicated on the chart. When the design is finished, cut 10 × 6-in (15.25-cm) lengths of embroidery thread and lay them along the inside openings of the shells, leaving equal tails of thread loose at each end. Squeeze a line of glue on the top of each shell opening, over the embroidery thread, and set aside to dry. When they are ready, take the two ends and thread them into holes nearest to the eight positions indicated on the chart. Tie securely at the back and cut off the waste ends.

Finishing

Take your completed embroidery and fold back the edges ½ in (12 mm). Position the panel at the centre of the bottom edge of your towel and hand sew or machine stitch it into position. Lay the towel in front of you, wrong side up, and fold the free end to form a 12-in (30.5-cm) deep pocket. Sew the side seams and make two further seams 6 in (15.25 cm) apart to form three channels in which to keep your bathroom accessories. Take the two remaining shells and thread the ends through the towel, positioning them approximately 1 in (2.5 cm) from the bottom of the two centre seams to act as buttons. With the crochet hook and two lengths of embroidery thread (see page 164), make two chains approximately 2 in (5 cm) long and use to form two loops at the other end of the towel to correspond with the shell buttons. Make two more chains of embroidery thread and attach them at the sides of the towel, level with the top of your embroidered panel. These can be used to hang your bag on a piece of dowelling, or on a hook in your bathroom.

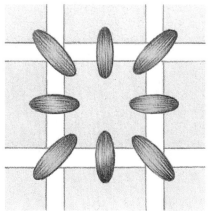
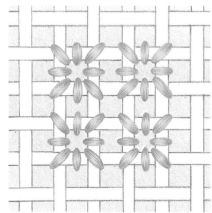

Star stitch is worked on a block of nine holes, working into each hole and back to the centre each time.

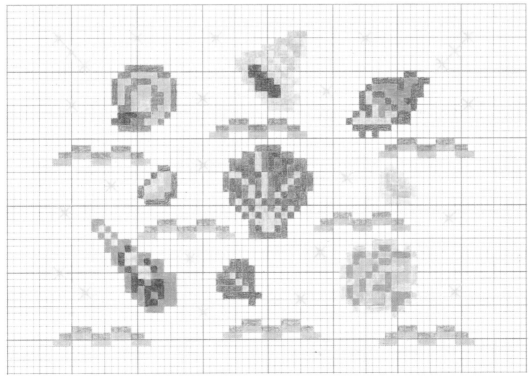

Shell Picture Frame

If you do not want to go the whole hog and embroider the stripes on this frame, you could work the motifs on paper canvas (perforated paper), cover a frame with striped fabric and glue your embroidery on the corner. For added interest, you could glue some real shells along the outside of the frame and incorporate one or two real cockle shells into the embroidered design.

Actual design measures:
10 × 9 in (25.4 × 22.9 cm)

Materials
1 piece of 14-count Aida measuring
12 × 11 in (30.5 × 28 cm)
2 pieces of mounting card (mat
board) each measuring 10 × 9 in
(25.4 × 22.9 cm)
No 8 crewel needle
Rubber-based adhesive
Scalpel or craft knife
Pencil

Anchor stranded cottons (floss):

1 skein of grey (233)
1 skein of grey (234)
1 skein of yellow (295)
1 skein of gold (362)
3 skeins of pale yellow (292)
3 skeins of turquoise (168)
1 skein of pink (868)
1 skein of rose (894)
1 skein of white (1)

Instructions
Count 14 holes in on the left side and 14 holes up from the bottom and begin here. Work the entire design in cross stitch using two strands of cotton (floss). When the design is complete, cut out the plain centre panel to within ½ in (12 mm) of your embroidery. Slit the corners carefully and fold back the waste canvas leaving a clean edge. Lay your finished work on top of one piece of mounting card (mat board) and draw around the inner square with a pencil. Cut this shape from the card with a scalpel. Fold back the edges of the canvas over the card, glueing them into position. Take care to check that the stripes remain straight. Lay the completed picture frame on top of the remaining piece of card and glue down the sides and bottom, leaving the top open to slide in your photograph.

The chart for the Shell Picture Frame is shown on pages 84–5.

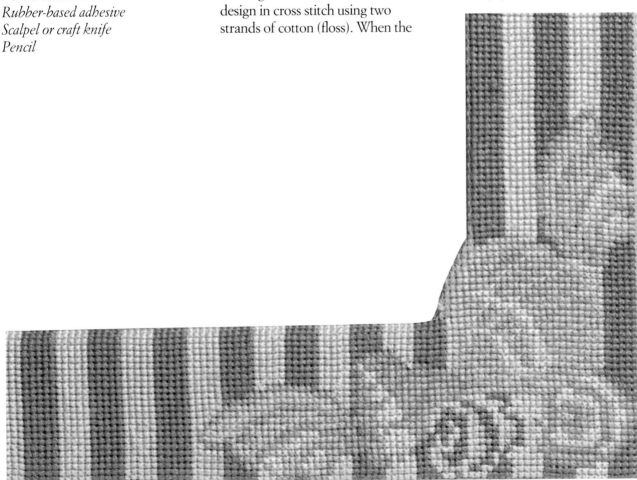

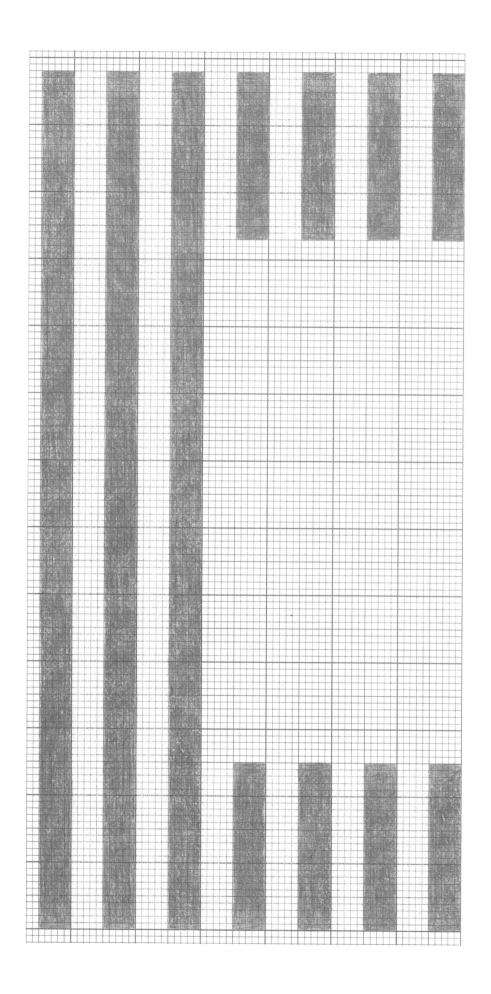

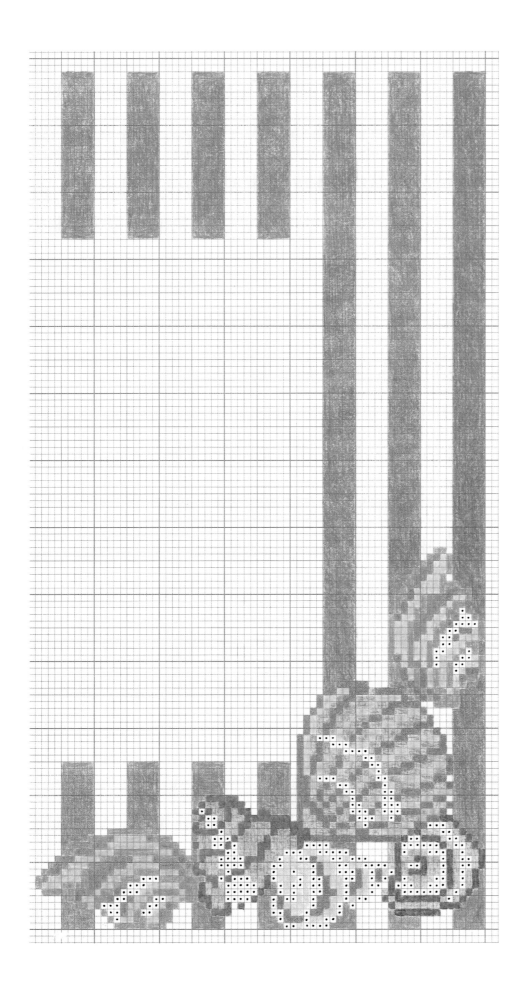

AMERICAN FOLK BATHROOM

We have many reasons to thank the eighteenth- and nineteenth-century homemakers of rural North America. Not only have they taught us a style of decoration which is timeless and practical, but the methods they used to achieve it have inspired craftspeople working in a vast array of mediums ever since.

From homespun patchworks to hand-painted furniture, the bold colours and stylized motifs typical of these communities have brightened our homes, and the simplicity of approach has shown that the desired end is not beyond our means.

Interpretations of boldly coloured birds and flowers and the traditional symbols of folk art are strangely universal. Many similar motifs can be found in the work of Eastern Europe, Asia and even Australasia, but it is perhaps the settlers of the Atlantic coast of North America who interpreted these motifs in a way that suggested the comfort and style that we still attempt to reproduce.

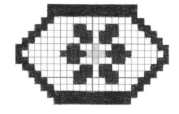

American Folk Sampler

This first project is a demonstration of how motifs and borders can be practised and at the same time arranged in a simple composition that warrants a frame in its own right. If you stitch because your creative instincts tell you to, put them into full flight and stitch simple motifs in your own choice of colours on to canvas. Start with one image, maybe a bird or a flower, and work it in different positions mirroring, re-colouring and reversing it. Add a brightly coloured border and an alphabet of your choice and before you know it you will have created a central theme for your room and a piece of work which is truly stamped with your own identity. The following piece of work is intended only as a guideline for you to begin with.

Actual design measures:
12 × 11½ in (30.5 × 29.2 cm)

Materials
One piece of 14-count Aida
  measuring 15 × 18 in
  (38 × 45.75 cm)
No 24 tapestry needle

Anchor stranded cottons (floss):

□ *1 skein of yellow (298)*
■ *1 skein of turquoise (410)*
□ *1 skein of green (227)*
■ *1 skein of red (29)*
□ *1 skein of pink (85)*
■ *2 skeins of fuchsia (89)*
□ *1 skein of blue (118)*

Instructions
Mark the centre of your chart and
the centre of your canvas. Using
three strands of cotton (floss), work
from here in cross stitch until the
design is complete. Frame (see the
techniques on page 161) according
to taste but keep it simple!

American Folk Cabinet

This little cabinet is ideal for collectors. In the bathroom you could use it to display shells, corals or pebbles or perhaps a collection of pill boxes. The central panel is worked on linen and you can of course use this idea with any piece of furniture that offers you a plain wooden panel begging for decoration. Mount your embroidery on lightweight cardboard and glue it into position.

Actual panel measures:
3½ in (8.9 cm) square
Actual design measures:
3 in (7.5 cm) square

Materials

Framecraft miniature cabinet (see stockists/suppliers information on page 165)
1 piece of 32-count linen measuring 5 in (12.7 cm) square
Lightweight cardboard
Glue
No 8 crewel needle

Anchor stranded cottons (floss):

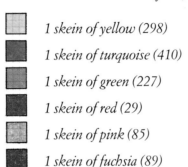

1 skein of yellow (298)
1 skein of turquoise (410)
1 skein of green (227)
1 skein of red (29)
1 skein of pink (85)
1 skein of fuchsia (89)

Instructions

Mark the centre of your chart and the centre of the linen. Using two strands of cotton (floss) over two strands of linen, work from here in cross stitch throughout. When the embroidery is complete, mount on cardboard following the manufacturer's instructions and glue to the panel in the cabinet.

The chart for the American Folk Sampler is shown on pages 88–9.

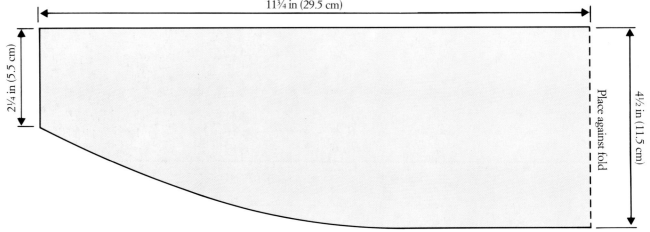

11¾ in (29.5 cm)

2¼ in (5.5 cm)

4½ in (11.5 cm)

Place against fold

American Folk Curtain Tie

This border pattern can be used for lots of different projects. You could use it as a frieze across a window blind (shade) or as an edging for a shelf or series of shelves. You could also display it vertically as a bell pull. Add or take away as many of the motifs as you please according to the size you require.

Actual design measures:
17 × 2½ in (43 × 6.3 cm)

Materials

1 piece of 11-count Aida measuring
*   20 × 5 in (51 × 12.7 cm)*
2 pieces of backing material (I have
*   used cotton chintz) each*
*   measuring 26 × 6 in (66 ×*
*   15.25 cm)*
1 piece of buckram measuring
*   24 × 4 in (61 × 10 cm)*
Plain paper
Pencil
No 24 tapestry needle
Small length of narrow ribbon for
*   loops*

Anchor stranded cottons (floss):

1 skein of yellow (298)

1 skein of turquoise (410)

1 skein of red (29)

1 skein of pink (85)

2 skeins of fuchsia (89)

Instructions

Leaving 1 in (2.5 cm) of Aida at the left edge and top and bottom, begin working from the chart, in cross stitch, using three strands of cotton (floss). Work the chart three times, then repeat the first block of eight stitches. Trace off the template on to paper. Fold the buckram in half and lay the template on top with the straight edge against the fold. Cut to size. Cut two pieces of backing fabric, approximately ½ in (12 mm) larger than the buckram all round. Sandwich the buckram in between, turn in and pin the waste edges of the backing and machine stitch or hand sew together, inserting two loops of ribbon at the centre of the short ends. Pin your embroidery along the centre of the tie, folding in the raw edges. Hand sew or machine stitch into position.

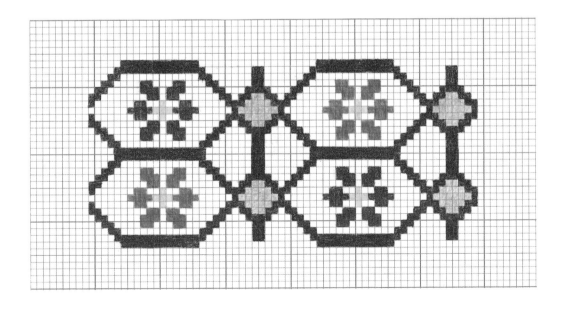

American Folk Hook Panel

This panel could be fixed to your bathroom door for your dressing gowns (bathrobes) or it could be used to hold towels. The wooden panel with hooks was bought ready-made but you could make your own with a strip of 2 × ½ in (2.5 cm × 12 mm) wood and some ornamental hooks.

Actual design measures:
12 × 4½ in (30.5 × 11.5 cm)

Materials
1 piece of 14-count Aida measuring
 15 × 18 in (38 × 45.7 cm)
1 piece of turquoise felt measuring
 16 × 11 in (40.6 × 28 cm)
1 piece of board measuring 14 × 9 in
 (35.5 × 22.9 cm)
1 piece of board measuring 13 × 5½
 in (33 × 14 cm)
1 piece of polyester wadding
 (synthetic batting) measuring
 13 × 5½ in (33 × 14 cm)
Rubber-based adhesive
No 24 tapestry needle

Anchor stranded cottons (floss):

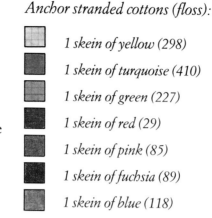

1 skein of yellow (298)

1 skein of turquoise (410)

1 skein of green (227)

1 skein of red (29)

1 skein of pink (85)

1 skein of fuchsia (89)

1 skein of blue (118)

Instructions
Mark the centre of your chart and the centre of your canvas. Using three strands of cotton (floss), work from here in cross stitch until the design is complete. Take the smaller of the two boards and glue your wadding (batting) on to the front. Stretch the embroidery over the padded board and glue the edges to the back. Glue the felt to the remaining board in the same way. Then glue your mounted embroidery on to the felt-covered panel, centring it 1 in (2.5 cm) down from the top.

If you have used battening, make screw holes at each end and screw on your hooks at equally spaced intervals. Glue to the board underneath the mounted embroidery. Screw to a wall or door through the holes made in the battening and through the felt panel.

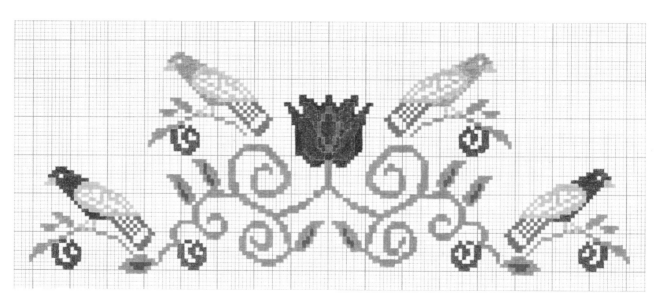

TOILE DE JOUY BATHROOM

The term toile de Jouy derives from fabrics produced in 1770 at the Jouy factory in the village of Jouy-en-Josas near Versailles in France. The original designs were created using the copper plate technique printed on to Indian calico and often depicted pastoral scenes and pictorial images. The factory was extremely successful and in 1806, the founder, German-born Christophe Philippe, set up a cotton mill in France with his brother.

The business advanced further by means of industrial espionage when the brothers visited England in 1810 to investigate various workshops and obtain information on machinery. This information was smuggled out of England through the use of invisible writing. Natural dyes were used to colour toile de Jouy, madder for the pinkish-red colours and indigo and woad for the blues, together with other vegetable dyes for the less popular colours. Many of the pictorial images that were featured were based on events of the time and therefore have historical significance.

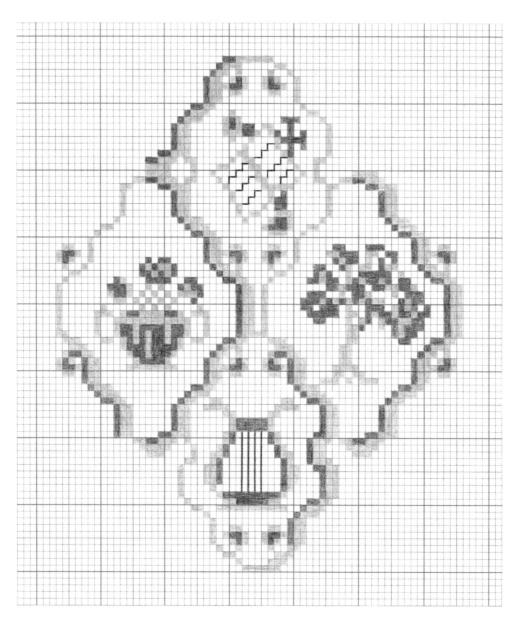

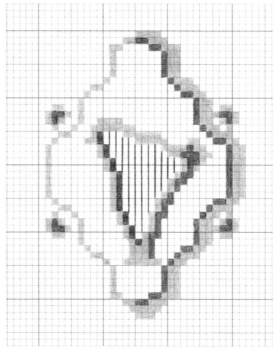

Toile de Jouy Brush and Mirror Set

This brush and mirror set is custom-made for embroidery but you may well find an old set at a flea market, car boot (yard) sale or auction. Silver-topped perfume bottles and crystal jars can also be bought with blank panels for embroidery and these provide a rich and interesting collection for the boudoir.

If you have a plain-backed mirror or brush with an interesting surround you could mount your cross stitch design on a piece of medium-weight cardboard and glue it to the back, but it is advisable to work your design on fine fabric to avoid bulkiness and creasing.

Actual design measures:
Mirror 5 × 4 in (12.7 × 10 cm);
Brush 2½ × 2 in (6.3 × 5 cm)

Materials

Framecraft silver brush and mirror set. This comes complete with a comb and can be bought at many good embroidery shops or by mail order (see the stockist/suppliers information on page 165)
For the mirror: one piece of 32-count Irish linen measuring 7 × 7½ in (17.8 × 19 cm)
For the brush: one piece of 32-count Irish linen measuring 5 × 6 in (12.7 × 15.25 cm)
No 8 crewel needle
Cardboard

FOR THE MIRROR:
Anchor stranded cottons (floss):

1 skein of blue (159)

1 skein of blue grey (849)

FOR THE BRUSH:
Anchor stranded cottons (floss):

1 skein of blue (159)

1 skein of blue grey (849)

Instructions

Mark the centre of the chart and the centre of the linen. Starting here, work in cross stitch and straight stitch as indicated on the charts. Use two strands of cotton (floss) and stitch over two threads of linen. When the design is complete, trim off the excess linen and mount on cardboard following the manufacturer's instructions.

Toile Candle Screen

This candle screen is custom-built to show off embroidery and demonstrates the many unusual items that can be transformed with your cross stitch skills. My stitchers particularly enjoyed making the projects in this section. Although they are produced on fine linen which requires a good light to work in, the fact that only two colours are used reduces the fiddly aspect and the end results are stunning. If you enjoy fine work, you might like to consider incorporating these design panels in a sampler or a firescreen. Of course, there is nothing to stop you working on a coarser fabric and speeding up the process. For details of where to buy the candle screen, turn to the stockists/suppliers information on page 165.

Actual design measures:
3½ × 2¾ in (8.9 × 7 cm)

Materials
Framecraft candle screen (see stockists/suppliers information on page 165)
1 piece of 32-count linen measuring 7 × 6 in (17.8 × 15.25 cm)
No 8 crewel needle

Anchor stranded cottons (floss):

 1 skein of moss green (843)

 1 skein of dark moss green (681)

Instructions
Mark the centre of the chart and the centre of your fabric and work from here in cross stitch and straight stitch as indicated on the chart. Use two strands of cotton (floss) and stitch over two threads of linen. When the design is complete, mount according to the manufacturer's instructions.

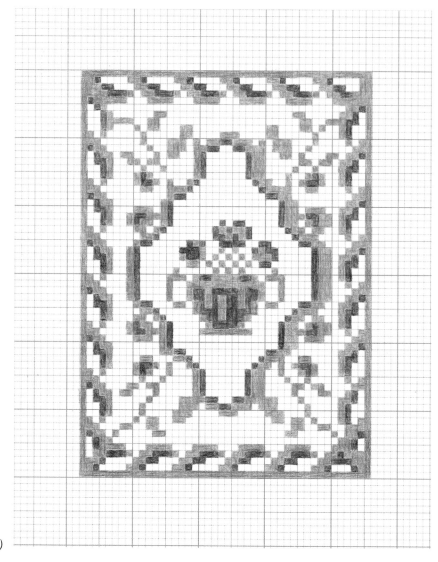

Toile de Jouy Guest Towel

This evenweave hand towel in soft ivory is the perfect background for the soft subtle pinks incorporated in this toile. The towels can be bought ready-fringed (see the stockists/suppliers information on page 165) or you might like to use your own cotton guest towel and work the design over waste canvas. The towel I have used has 26 holes to the inch and should be embroidered over two threads of fabric in both directions. You can adjust the width by adding or subtracting lozenges or you might like to use this design as a border for a curtain or curtain tie back. You could also work the lozenges vertically as opposed to horizontally and create a bell pull.

Actual design measures:
12 × 4¾ in (30.5 × 12 cm)

Materials

1 evenweave guest towel measuring 15 in (38 cm) wide
No 7 crewel needle

Anchor stranded cottons (floss):

 3 skeins of pink (893)

2 skeins of rose (895)

Instructions

Mark the centre of your chart and, allowing a plain border of approximately 2 in (5 cm), mark the centre of the towel. Work the design from here in cross stitch and straight stitch as indicated on the chart. Use three strands of cotton (floss) and stitch over two threads of fabric. You can create your own towel using Linda fabric which is available in numerous colours and counts. To create a quality appearance, however, I would suggest that you hand-roll and stitch the side edges.

Bedrooms

FLOWERS AND LACE BEDROOM

Use these pretty wildflower motifs to decorate a lace bedroom. These cushion covers and the bedspread lend themselves perfectly to embroidery as the panels allow you to work as many or as few flowers as you wish (see the stockists/suppliers information on page 165). You can pick up lots of lace-trimmed items at auctions, car boot and jumble (yard) sales. Embroider a single wild flower on the corner of your pillowcase or dot them over the turn-back on your sheet.

Lace Bedspread

This pretty bedspread is perfect for a bedroom. You can work more or fewer panels as you wish.

Actual designs measure: approximately 1½ in (3.8 cm) square

Materials

Lace panelled bedspread measuring 72 × 90 in (183 × 229 cm)
42 pieces of 15-count waste canvas, each measuring 2½ in (6.3 cm) square
Contrasting sewing thread for tacking (basting)
No 8 crewel needle
Pair of tweezers

Anchor stranded cottons (floss):

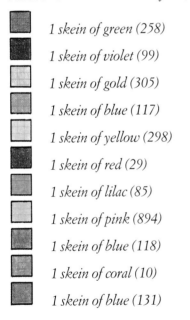

1 skein of green (258)
1 skein of violet (99)
1 skein of gold (305)
1 skein of blue (117)
1 skein of yellow (298)
1 skein of red (29)
1 skein of lilac (85)
1 skein of pink (894)
1 skein of blue (118)
1 skein of coral (10)
1 skein of blue (131)

Instructions

Working across the width of the bedspread, tack (baste) the squares of waste canvas to the cotton squares of the bedspread, working from right to left and positioning them as follows:

Row 1: the first square then the two following fourth squares.
Row 2: the third square then the two following fourth squares.
Row 3 and every alternate row: as Row 1.
Row 4 and every alternate row: as Row 2.

Continue in this sequence until every row has waste canvas stitched into place.

Using two strands of cotton (floss) work the motifs from the chart in cross stitch, working over two threads of canvas. Work in this sequence: rose, lavender, scarlet pimpernel, blue daisy, harebell, primrose, forget-me-not, heartsease. Then repeat from the beginning. When all the motifs have been stitched, carefully remove the waste canvas from under the embroidery with tweezers. Add straight stitch detail as indicated on the charts.

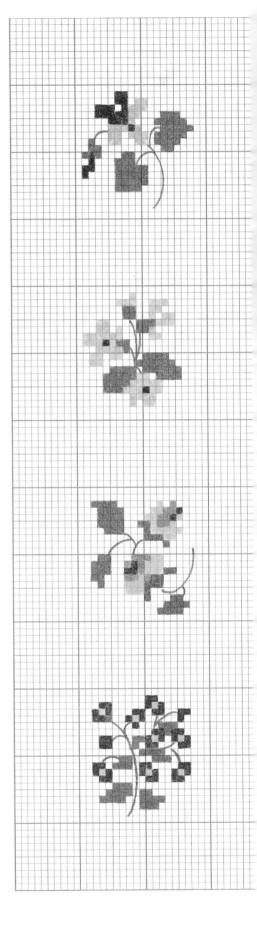

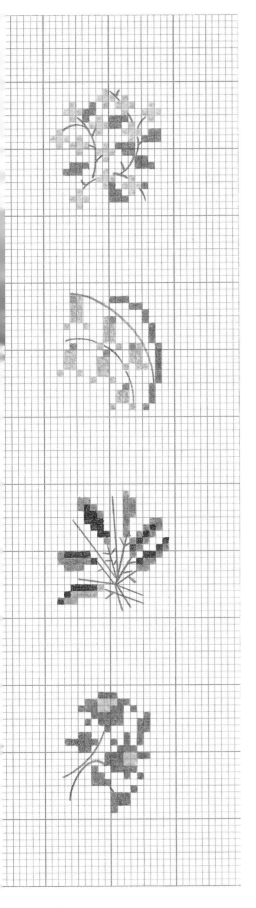

Wild Flower Cushion

This cushion uses the same motifs as the Lace Bedspread, so is the ideal companion for it.

Actual design measures: approximately 1½ in (3.8 cm) square

Materials

1 lace and cotton panelled cushion, measuring 16 in (40.6 cm) square (see the stockists/suppliers information on page 165)
16 pieces of 15-count waste canvas, each measuring 2½ in (6.3 cm) square
No 8 crewel needle
Pair of tweezers

Anchor stranded cottons (floss):

1 skein of green (258)
1 skein of violet (99)
1 skein of gold (305)
1 skein of blue (117)
1 skein of yellow (298)
1 skein of red (29)
1 skein of lilac (85)
1 skein of pink (894)
1 skein of blue (118)
1 skein of coral (10)
1 skein of blue (131)

Instructions

Tack (baste) the waste canvas to the centre of each plain square of cotton on the cushion cover. Mark the centre of each chart and of each square of waste canvas. Starting here, work the eight charts over eight squares and then repeat for the second set of eight squares. Work in cross stitch using two strands of cotton (floss) over two threads of canvas. When every square is complete, carefully remove the waste canvas from underneath the embroidery with tweezers. Add stems in straight stitch, using two strands of cotton, as indicated on the charts.

Rose and Forget-Me-Not Cushion

This design is worked on a larger version of the panelled cushion and features small posies of roses and forget-me-nots. I have chosen to place the design on every second square but you can, of course, work on every square if preferred. Alternatively, you could repeat one of the motifs from the Wild Flower Cushion (the heartsease or primroses would work well) on every alternate square.

Actual design measures:
2¼ × 2 in (5.7 × 5 cm)

Materials

1 lace and cotton panelled cushion, measuring 22 in (55.8 cm) square (see stockists/suppliers information on page 165)
8 pieces of 15-count waste canvas, each measuring 3 in (7.5 cm) square
No 8 crewel needle
Pair of tweezers

Anchor stranded cottons (floss):

1 skein of green (255)
1 skein of blue (118)
1 skein of yellow (298)
1 skein of peach (893)
1 skein of coral (10)
1 skein of rose (894)
1 skein of red (13)

Instructions

Tack (baste) the waste canvas to the centre of every alternate plain square of cotton on the cushion cover. Mark the centre of each chart and of each square of waste canvas. Starting here, work each motif from the chart using two strands of cotton (floss), working in cross stitch over two threads of canvas. When the motifs are complete, carefully remove the waste canvas from under the embroidery using tweezers. Add stems in straight stitch using two strands of cotton.

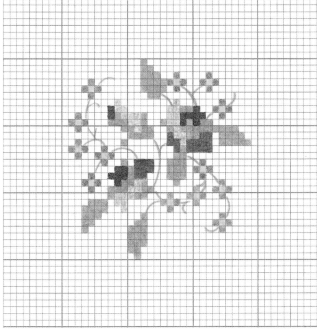

Spring Bouquet Heart

This little heart is designed for use as a pot pourri sachet. The hearts can be bought in two separate halves, ready for embroidery (see the stockists/suppliers information on page 165), or you could make your own from some white cotton or linen and lace trim. The spring bouquet could be used together with an initial (see pages 116–17) to decorate the corner of a pillowcase, or repeated continuously as a border for a photoframe. If you choose this last option edge the design with two or three rows of plain cross stitch in the blue or the pink.

Actual design measures:
2¼ × 2 in (5.7 × 5 cm)

Materials

*Either a ready-made cotton and lace heart (see stockists/suppliers information on page 165) or 2 pieces of white cotton or linen, each measuring 6 in (15.25 cm) square and 1 yard (90 cm) of 1-in (2.5-cm) wide lace trimming
1 piece of 15-count waste canvas, measuring 3 in (7.5 cm) square
White sewing thread
No 8 crewel needle
Pair of tweezers
Dried lavender flowers or pot pourri*

Anchor stranded cottons (floss):

- 1 skein of green (256)
- 1 skein of blue (128)
- 1 skein of yellow (305)
- 1 skein of peach (4146)
- 1 skein of pink (26)
- 1 skein of blue (131)
- 1 skein of orange (330)
- 1 skein of white (1)
- 1 skein of cherry (19)
- 1 skein of pink (28)

Instructions

If you are making up a heart yourself, take a 6-in (15.25-cm) square piece of paper and fold it in half. Draw half a heart shape with the centre against the fold and cut it out. Pin the paper heart on to your fabric and cut out two pieces. Using white cotton sewing thread, work in buttonhole stitch around the edges of both heart shapes to protect from fraying. Set one heart aside and tack the waste canvas to the centre of the other. Work the design from the chart in cross stitch, using two strands of cotton (floss) and working over two threads of canvas. When the design is complete, carefully remove the waste canvas from underneath the embroidery with tweezers. Using two strands of cotton, work the detail in straight stitch as indicated on the chart.

Finishing

Leaving two 2-in (5-cm) ends of lace centre top, pin then tack (baste) the lace all around the embroidered heart, stitching it close to the edge at the back. Place the second heart behind the first and stitch together, so sandwiching the lace in between the two hearts. Leave a small opening at the top, insert your pot pourri then finish off the seam. Join the two tails of lace to form a loop for hanging.

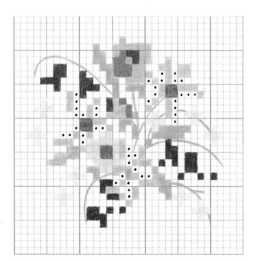

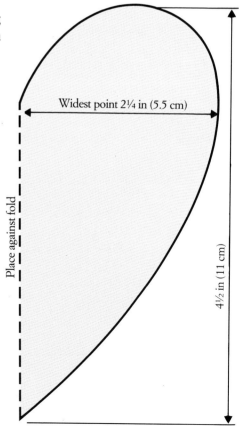

Widest point 2¼ in (5.5 cm)

Place against fold

4½ in (11 cm)

Little Rose Heart

This is worked in exactly the same way as the Spring Bouquet Heart except that I have used a motif from the Lace Bedspread/Wild Flower Cushion. It would be particularly appropriate to fill this heart with dried rose petals. If you don't want to use a special pot pourri, take a small piece of wadding (batting) and sprinkle on a few drops of your favourite essential oil. Place this inside the heart instead of the flower petals.

Actual design measures:
1½ in (3.8 cm) square

Materials
1 cotton and lace heart (see Spring Bouquet Heart)
1 piece of 15-count waste canvas, measuring 2 in (5 cm) square
No 8 crewel needle
Sewing thread for tacking (basting)

Anchor stranded cottons (floss):

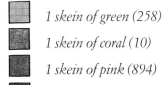

■ *1 skein of green (258)*
■ *1 skein of coral (10)*
■ *1 skein of pink (894)*
■ *1 skein of red (29)*

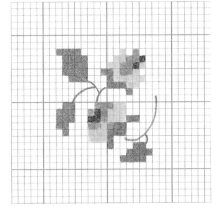

Instructions
Follow the instructions for the Spring Bouquet Heart (see page 112).

BUTTERFLIES AND MONOGRAMS BEDROOM

Given the time it takes to complete an embroidery, a personal signature really is in order and numerous books on alphabets are available to enable you to come up with your very own trademark. Take the initial of your name and place it next to your favourite motif, or work your motif into your initial to create a complete picture. Samplers worked in Victorian England nearly always used alphabets as a central theme and, after creating a model of the 26 letters in stitches, messages, mottos and proverbs were embroidered in the same style.

As a result, traditional samplers look charming in traditional decors and the following lettering charts can be used either as one complete image in sampler form or in isolation. I have based my alphabet on a classic script but do not be limited either by my choice of lettering style or my butterfly motifs since, with some tracing paper and a little imagination, you can personalize any item in your own special style.

Butterfly Sampler

For this project I charted an alphabet and, as an afterthought, decided to create a butterfly border using a mixture of colours and positions. Given the nature of the creatures, it was inevitable that one or two would fly into the main body of the design and make their presence known.

Actual design measures:
12 × 15½ in (30.5 × 39.5 cm)

Materials
1 piece of 18-count Aida measuring
*   15 × 18 in (38 × 45.75 cm)*
No 8 crewel needle

Anchor stranded cottons (floss):

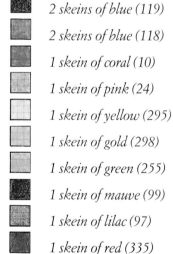

2 skeins of blue (119)
2 skeins of blue (118)
1 skein of coral (10)
1 skein of pink (24)
1 skein of yellow (295)
1 skein of gold (298)
1 skein of green (255)
1 skein of mauve (99)
1 skein of lilac (97)
1 skein of red (335)
1 skein of yellow (293)
1 skein of brown (936)

Instructions
Mark the centre of your chart (see pages 116–17) and the centre of your fabric. Work from here in cross stitch using two strands of cotton (floss) and working over two threads of linen. Work butterfly antennae in straight stitch. Frame to your requirements (see page 161).

Nightdress Case with Monogram

One of my favourite occupations is to hunt through bundles of household fabrics at car boot (yard) sales and auctions in the hope that a beautiful piece of hand-made lace work will surface. It is therefore very unsporting of many department stores to stock hand-made, lace-trimmed linen and cotton whatnots that look exactly like the real thing but have in fact been produced just a few weeks ago. My nightdress case with its lace edging and insets is in fact one of those newly born pieces and as such benefitted from the authentic hand stitching that has been added. If you have an old lace dressing-table set or runner, you can easily make a similar item yourself by backing it with a strip of cotton, the same width but double the length of your worked piece, which should be folded in two and seamed at the sides to form a bag. Your finished embroidery should then be tacked (basted) to the top back edge of this bag so that it forms a flap.

If you have a long narrow runner made from linen or cotton and lace, simply fold it in three, turn the top third over and add an initial and a motif. Pieces of lace and cotton can be salvaged to make all kinds of pretty bedroom accessories, from tissue cases to box tops. Do not discard old fabrics because they are torn or stained, just cut away the offending area and think creatively about what is left.

Actual design measures:
3 × 2½ in (7.5 × 6.3 cm)

Materials
Old lace pochette (bag) or
*   lace-trimmed square plus twice*
*   the length of cotton or linen fabric*
1 piece of 15-count waste canvas
*   measuring 4 in (10 cm) square*
White sewing thread
No 8 crewel needle
Pair of tweezers

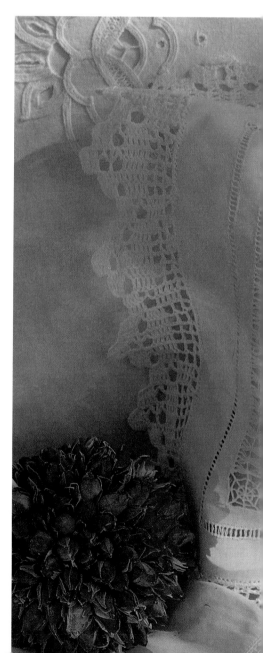

Anchor stranded cottons (floss):

- 1 *skein of pink (24)*
- 1 *skein of coral (10)*
- 1 *skein of green (255)*
- 1 *skein of lilac (97)*
- 1 *skein of green (233)*
- 1 *skein of blue (119)*
- 1 *skein of blue (118)*
- 1 *skein of yellow (293)*

Instructions

Tack (baste) the waste canvas to the centre of the lace-trimmed square. Select and trace off your charted initial and position the butterfly to hover over the posy of flowers. Mark the centre of your chart and the centre of the waste canvas and work in cross stitch from here, using two strands of cotton (floss) over two threads of canvas. When the design is complete, carefully remove the waste canvas from underneath the embroidery with tweezers. Add the butterfly's antennae using straight stitches.

If you are making up your own pouch, fold your strip of cotton in two and sew up the side seams. Stitch the embroidered square to the top back edge to form a flap.

Monogram Sachet

Small sachets make lovely gifts and can be used to decorate and perfume a bedroom. They also provide you with a good use for leftover pieces of embroidery fabric and thread. Back them with scraps of curtaining fabric for a co-ordinated look and trim with ribbon and lace.

Actual design measures:
4½ × 2½ in (11.5 × 6.3 cm)

Materials

*1 piece of 30-count linen measuring
   5½ × 3½ in (14 × 8.9 cm)
1 piece of backing fabric measuring
   5½ × 3½ in (14 × 8.9 cm)
1 piece of wadding (batting)
   measuring 10 × 5 in
   (25.4 × 12.7 cm), perfumed with
   a few drops of essential oil
1 piece of lace ¾ in (19 mm) wide ×
   29½ in (75 cm) long
1 piece of ribbon ¾ in (19 mm) wide
   × 29½ in (75 cm) long
4 ribbon bows
White sewing thread
No 8 crewel needle*

Anchor stranded cottons (floss):

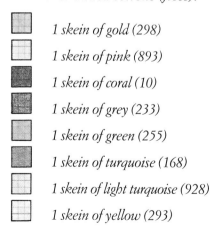

- 1 skein of gold (298)
- 1 skein of pink (893)
- 1 skein of coral (10)
- 1 skein of grey (233)
- 1 skein of green (255)
- 1 skein of turquoise (168)
- 1 skein of light turquoise (928)
- 1 skein of yellow (293)

Instructions

Select and trace off the chosen initials from the chart and position a butterfly nearby. Do not use the flower motif on the second initial but continue the line of the letter instead. Mark the centre of your chart and the centre of the linen and work the design in cross stitch using two strands of cotton (floss) over two threads of linen. Complete the butterfly motif by adding the antennae in straight stitches.

When the embroidery is finished pin it to your backing fabric, turning in approximately ¼ in (6 mm) all round both the back and front edges. Stitch together along the bottom and sides, fold the perfumed wadding (batting) in two and insert in the top, then join along the top seam. Tack (baste) lace and ribbon around the outer edge and add a bow on each corner.

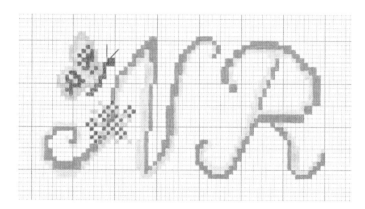

Pillowcase with Monogram

Add an initial to a pillowcase or the corner of the turn-back of a sheet. You could also decorate a plain white duvet cover with butterflies or make a sampler using just the butterfly motifs in different colours and frame it so it looks like a collection of the real things.

Actual design measures: approximately 3 in (7.5 cm) square depending on the initial chosen

Materials
Plain white pillowcase
1 piece of 15-count waste canvas measuring 4 in (10 cm) square
No 8 crewel needle
Sewing thread for tacking (basting)
Pair of tweezers

Anchor stranded cottons (floss):

1 skein of coral (10)
1 skein of pink (24)
1 skein of yellow (295)
1 skein of blue (118)
1 skein of blue (119)
1 skein of grey (233)
1 skein of green (255)

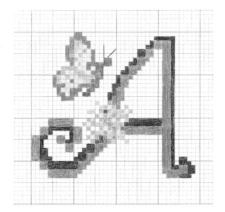

Instructions
Tack (baste) your waste canvas at an angle on the corner of your pillowcase. Select and trace your initial, positioning a butterfly over the posy of flowers. Mark the centre of your chart and the centre of the waste canvas. Starting here, work in cross stitch using two strands of cotton (floss) over two threads of canvas. When your design is complete, carefully remove the waste canvas from under the embroidery with a pair of tweezers.

CUPIDS AND ROSES BEDROOM

Cupid or Amorino fits perfectly into a bedroom setting because he has been identified by the Greeks as Eros, god of love, and by the Romans as the son of Venus. It is not quite clear who his father was – some believe him to be Jupiter, others Mars or Mercury – but this chubby little cherub certainly played a very important role in the art and architecture of the Renaissance and Baroque periods and he is currently enjoying a popular revival. Cupid's leaden arrow is the symbol of sensual love, while his golden arrow symbolizes virtuous love. He is often depicted in art and sculpture carrying a bow and arrow or strewn with garlands of flowers like the winged celestial spirit featured in the following projects.

Swag of Roses

This small swag of roses is used here to decorate a detail on a square of tape lace which is then folded in half to form an oblong cushion. It can also be repeated as a border for a pillowcase or worked as a mirror image for a photo frame. Worked on a piece of canvas with fewer holes to the inch, you could use the swag as a curtain tie back for plain lace curtains.

Actual design measures:
5 × 2 in (12.7 × 5 cm)

Materials

1 piece of cotton lace measuring
16 in (40.6 cm) square
1 cushion pad or roll of polyester
wadding (synthetic batting) 16 in
(40.6 cm) long
1 piece of 15-count waste canvas
measuring 6 × 4 in
(15.25 × 10 cm)
White sewing thread
No 8 crewel needle
Pair of tweezers

Anchor stranded cottons (floss):

1 skein of fuchsia (28)

1 skein of pink (55)

1 skein of green (203)

Instructions

Tack (baste) the waste canvas into the required position on the lace square. Mark the centre of the chart and the centre of the waste canvas.

Starting here, work the design in cross stitch using two strands of cotton (floss) over two threads of canvas. When the embroidery is complete, carefully remove the strands of waste canvas from underneath the embroidery with the tweezers.

Fold the lace square in two over the cushion pad or roll of wadding (batting) and join at the side and bottom edges.

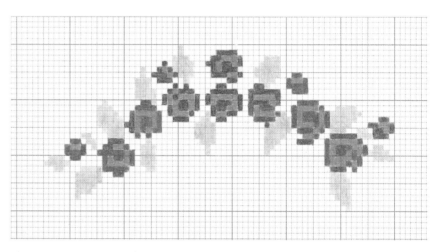

Cupid on Paper Canvas

There are numerous uses for embroidered motifs worked on paper canvas. They can be glued to screens to add special interest to a découpage (scrap paper) project. They are effective hung from a tree as Christmas decorations, worked as bookmarks and greetings cards, backed and hung as mobiles, or used in this way as an isolated motif cut to shape and glued to a picture or mirror frame.

Actual design measures:
5½ × 5 in (14 × 12.7 cm)

Materials

1 piece of 14-count perforated paper canvas, measuring 7 in (17.8 cm) square
1 reel (spool) of Kreinik Ombre Silver 1000
No 7 crewel needle
Rubber-based adhesive
Small pair of sharp pointed tip scissors

Anchor stranded cottons (floss):

- *1 skein of yellow (305)*
- *1 skein of gold (298)*
- *1 skein of red (335)*
- *1 skein of dark flesh (893)*
- *1 skein of flesh (4146)*
- *1 skein of blue (131)*
- *1 skein of light blue (130)*
- *1 skein of fuchsia (28)*
- *1 skein of pink (55)*
- *1 skein of green (203)*
- *1 reel of Kreinik Silver (see left)*

Instructions

Mark the centre of the chart (see bottom of page 128) and the centre of the paper canvas. Starting here, work in cross stitch using three strands of cotton (floss), but only two strands of silver thread for the wings. When the design is complete, cut away the square paper around Cupid, taking care not to cut into a hole in which a stitch is worked. Finish off the ends at the back of the work and glue them down with a rubber-based adhesive. Glue to the mirror or photo frame of your choice.

Cupid Jewellery Holder

Here is a neat way to display your jewellery and decorate your dressing table. The side panels are attached with tape to form mock hinges and, while I have covered them with satin, you could use lace, leftover curtaining or any fabric that takes your fancy. Stitch lengths of ribbon on to the side boards to tie on your jewellery, as shown in the photograph.

Actual design measures:
6 × 7½ in (15.25 × 19 cm)

Materials
1 piece of 14-count Aida measuring
    12 × 9½ in (30.5 × 24 cm)
2 pieces of satin or other covering
    fabric, each measuring
    12 × 5½ in (30.5 × 14 cm)
2 pieces of polyester wadding
    (synthetic batting), each
    measuring 10 × 3½ in
    (25.4 × 8.9 cm)
1 piece of polyester wadding
    (synthetic batting) measuring
    10 × 7½ in (25.4 × 19 cm)
2 pieces of cardboard, each
    measuring 10 × 3½ in
    (25.4 × 8.9 cm)
1 piece of cardboard measuring
    10 × 7½ in (25.4 × 19 cm)
1 piece of felt measuring 13 × 10 in
    (33 × 25.4 cm)
Clean towel
Heavy-duty tape 2 in (5 cm) wide
    (carpet tape is ideal)
Rubber-based adhesive
1 reel (spool) of Kreinik Ombre
    Silver 1000
No 7 crewel needle
1¼ yards (1 metre) of ¼-in (8-mm)
    wide satin ribbon

Anchor stranded cottons (floss):

1 skein of yellow (305)
1 skein of gold (298)
1 skein of red (335)
1 skein of dark flesh (893)
2 skeins of flesh (4146)
1 skein of blue (131)
1 skein of light blue (130)
1 skein of fuchsia (28)
1 skein of pink (55)
1 skein of green (203)
1 reel of Kreinik Silver (see left)

Instructions
Mark the centre of the chart (made up of the two Cupids on page 128 joined together) and the centre of the Aida. Starting here, work the design in cross stitch using three strands of cotton (floss). Work the wings using two strands of silver thread. When the design is complete take your three pieces of cardboard and on each piece glue a corresponding piece of polyester wadding (synthetic batting). Centre your finished embroidery face up over the largest piece of padded cardboard and glue the waste edges to the back. Cover the two remaining pieces of padded cardboard with satin or furnishing fabric in the same way. Lay the three covered boards face down on a clean towel and line them up with the embroidered board in the centre. Leaving enough slack in the middle to allow the side boards to bend inwards, join the side boards to the middle board with two vertical strips of heavy-duty tape. Finally, glue your piece of felt over the three boards to hide the seams.

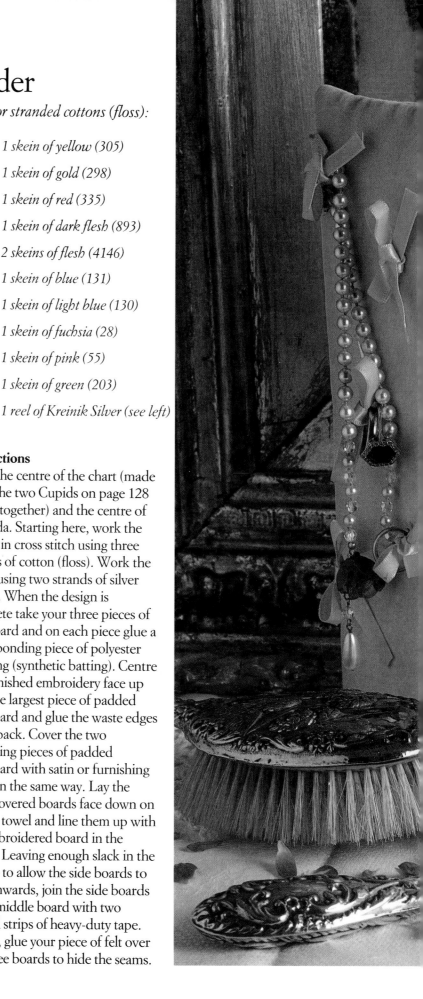

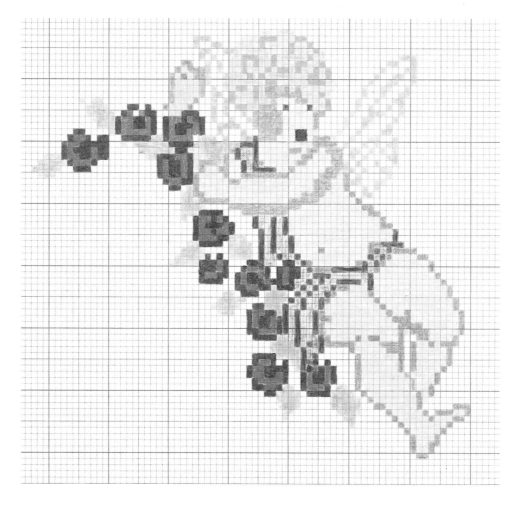

Cupid Runner

For this project I have worked Cupid horizontally to make him look as if he is flying (see the top chart on the facing page). This piece of embroidery is worked on the centre panel of a tray cloth, which can be used on a dressing table. If you prefer, you can back the tray cloth with fabric to form a cushion or drape it over a chair back. If you use it as a cushion, make it smell sweet by adding a sachet of pot pourri with the padding.

Actual design measures:
6 × 4 in (15.25 × 10 cm)

Materials
1 lace and cotton tray cloth measuring 20 × 13 in (51 × 33 cm) – see stockists/suppliers information on page 165
1 piece of 15-count waste canvas measuring 7 × 5 in (17.8 × 12.7 cm)
1 reel (spool) of Kreinik Ombre Silver 1000
Sewing thread for tacking (basting)
No 8 crewel needle
Pair of tweezers

Anchor stranded cottons (floss):

- *1 skein of yellow (305)*
- *1 skein of gold (298)*
- *1 skein of red (335)*
- *1 skein of dark flesh (893)*
- *2 skeins of flesh (4146)*
- *1 skein of blue (131)*
- *1 skein of light blue (130)*
- *1 skein of fuchsia (28)*
- *1 skein of pink (55)*
- *1 skein of green (203)*
- *1 reel of Kreinik Silver (see left)*

Instructions
Tack (baste) the waste canvas to the centre of the tray cloth. Mark the centre of the chart (see the top of page 128) and the centre of the waste canvas. Starting here, work in cross stitch using two strands of cotton or silver thread over two threads of canvas. When the design is complete, carefully remove the strands of waste canvas from under the embroidery with the tweezers.

Living Rooms

MIX AND MATCH LIVING ROOM

This section is intended to encourage you to produce your own designs from the fabrics, wallpapers and china in your home. I have used a Limoges dish and an old Royal Cauldon tea plate as inspiration and, having transferred sections of the designs into charts, have used the motifs as decorations for table linen, a cushion cover and a bell pull. Short-cuts to designing and creating your own charts are explained in the techniques section (see pages 158–64) and, having grasped the principle, you will find you can transform all your favourite images into cross stitch designs that will happily mix and match.

Limoges Cloth

This 14-in (35.5-cm) square of linen, edged in tape lace, was made in modern China. You could use it as a centre piece on a dining table or as a cloth for an occasional table. Alternatively, you could back it with white linen and turn it into a cushion. The design is taken from the centre panel of my dish which also has a pretty painted cartouche in gold which would not interpret well into cross stitch. Very crafty souls could paint on the gold detail using fabric paint or embroider it in satin stitch with gold thread.

Actual design measures:
6¾ × 2½ in (17.1 × 6.3 cm)

Materials

1 piece of lace-edged linen
measuring 14 in (35.5 cm) square
2 pieces of 15-count waste canvas
each measuring 7½ × 3 in
(19 × 7.5 cm)
Contrasting sewing thread for
tacking (basting)
No 8 crewel needle
Pair of tweezers

Anchor stranded cottons (floss):

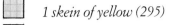

1 skein of yellow (295)
1 skein of rust (326)
1 skein of green (229)
1 skein of green (255)
1 skein of pink (85)
1 skein of flesh (4146)
1 skein of rose (77)
1 skein of blue (118)
1 skein of mauve (109)
1 skein of black (403)

Instructions

Position your waste canvas on the cloth approximately 3 in (7.5 cm) in from the borders. Tack (baste) the two strips in place using your contrasting thread. Mark the centre of the charts (noting the mirror image) and the centre of your waste canvas and, starting here, work the design in cross stitch using two strands of cotton (floss) over two threads of canvas. When the design is complete, carefully pull the strands of waste canvas from under the embroidery with the tweezers.

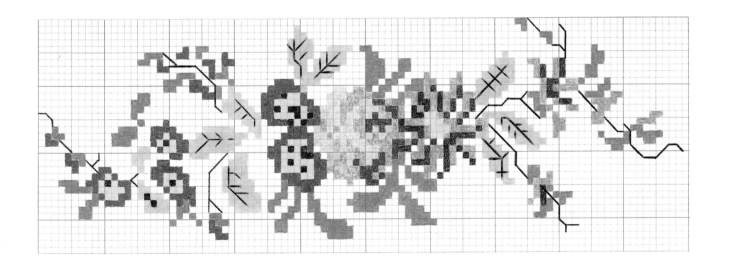

Mix and Match Bell Pull

You could work a bell pull in either of my two designs or make your own. The long narrow shape of the fabric lends itself to repeat border designs and a wallpaper frieze would provide the perfect inspiration for this project. I have taken separate floral motifs from my tea plate and re-arranged them with the use of mirror imaging to form a panel.

Actual design measures:
14½ × 3½ in (36.8 × 8.9 cm)

Materials
1 piece of 14-count Aida measuring 18 × 5 in (45.7 × 12.7 cm)
1 piece of backing fabric 1½ in (3.8 cm) longer than the Aida
1¼ yards (1 metre) of satin cord
1 bell
Sewing thread to match backing fabric
No 24 tapestry needle

Anchor stranded cottons (floss):

- *1 skein of yellow (295)*
- *1 skein of blue (118)*
- *1 skein of green (279)*
- *1 skein of dark pink (57)*
- *1 skein of purple (101)*
- *1 skein of medium pink (55)*
- *1 skein of gold (298)*
- *1 skein of lavender (119)*
- *1 skein of green (258)*
- *1 skein of rust (326)*
- *1 skein of light pink (23)*
- *1 skein of light blue (130)*

Instructions
Mark the centre of the chart and the centre of the Aida. Starting here, work the design in cross stitch using three strands of cotton (floss). When the design is complete, lay it face up on top of your backing fabric. Allow an extra 1 in (2.5 cm) of backing fabric at the top and an extra ½ in (12 mm) at the bottom. Turn in all side edges for approximately ½ in (12 mm) and sew together. Turn the backing fabric and Aida under at the bottom edge, leaving a small ridge of backing fabric showing at the front (see picture). Stitch together. Turn under the Aida at the top then **turn down** the backing fabric. **Stitch** together, leaving openings at **the side** through which to thread **your** cord. Thread the cord and tie **on the** bell.

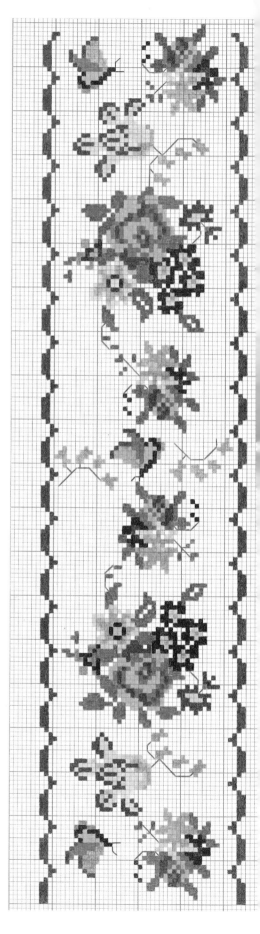

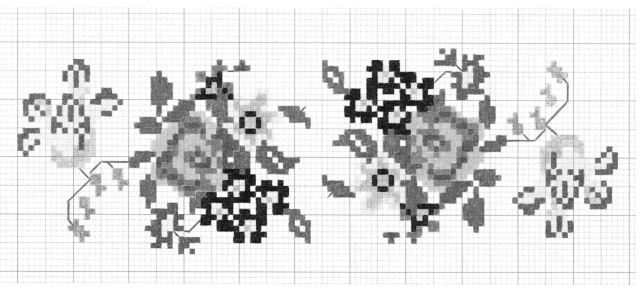

Mix and Match Bolster

I have used a ready-made bolster for this design but you could make one yourself very easily. Pads for bolsters are available from most good furnishing or department stores and you can make the cover from linen, sheeting or a piece of antique lace. The following instructions are for a plain cover which you could decorate with ribbon ties at either end.

Actual design measures:
7½ × 2¾ in (19 × 7 cm)

Materials
1 piece of linen measuring
*   33 × 34 in (83.8 × 86.3 cm)*
2 lengths of 1-in (2.5-cm) wide
*   ribbon approximately 27½ in*
*   (69.8cm) long*
1 piece of 15-count waste canvas
*   measuring 9½ × 4 in*
*   (24 × 10 cm)*
Sewing thread to match fabric
No 8 crewel needle
Pair of tweezers

Anchor stranded cottons (floss):

1 skein of yellow (295)
1 skein of blue (118)
1 skein of light green (279)
1 skein of dark pink (57)
1 skein of medium pink (55)
1 skein of gold (298)
1 skein of lavender (119)
1 skein of green (258)
1 skein of rust (326)
1 skein of light pink (23)
1 skein of light blue (130)

Instructions
Sew ½ in (12 mm) hems on the two shorter edges of fabric. Find the centre of the fabric and tack the waste canvas in position down the centre. Mark the centre of the chart and the centre of the canvas. Starting here, work the design in cross stitch using two strands of cotton (floss) over two threads of canvas. When the design is complete, carefully remove the strands of canvas from under the embroidery using tweezers. Fold the embroidery in half, right sides together, and join 1 in (2.5 cm) from the raw edges. Turn back the right way, insert the pad and gather both ends, tying them with ribbon bows.

Mix and Match Tablecloth

Take a plain or patterned tablecloth and work small motifs randomly or group them to complement a lace design. If you are working on a plain cloth, edge it with a one-colour, two-row border and create a panel in the centre by stitching a border. Alternatively, select single flower heads and dot them on to the cloth. Why not make up some napkins to match as well?

Actual designs measure:
1½ in (3.8 cm) square and
4 in (10 cm) square

Materials
1 square tablecloth
4 pieces of 15-count waste canvas
  each measuring 2½ in (6.3 cm)
  square
1 piece of 15-count waste canvas
  measuring 6½ in (16.5 cm) square
Contrasting sewing thread for
  tacking (basting)
No 8 crewel needle
Pair of tweezers

Anchor stranded cottons (floss):

1 skein of yellow (295)
1 skein of blue (118)
1 skein of green (279)
1 skein of dark pink (57)
1 skein of purple (101)
1 skein of medium pink (55)
1 skein of gold (298)
1 skein of lavender (119)
1 skein of green (258)
1 skein of rust (326)
1 skein of light pink (23)

Instructions
Position the four smallest pieces of waste canvas approximately 10 in (25.4 cm) in from each corner of the tablecloth with the vertical lines on the canvas pointing towards the corners. Tack (baste) in position. Centre the large panel of waste canvas and tack into position. Mark the centre of each piece of waste canvas and the centre of the charts. Start here, working in cross stitch using two strands of cotton (floss) over two threads of canvas. When all the charts have been completed, carefully remove the threads of canvas from under the embroidery with the tweezers.

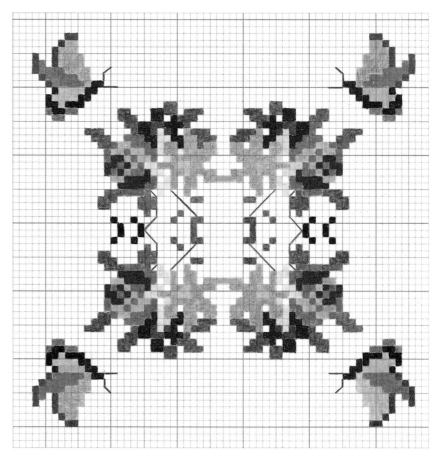

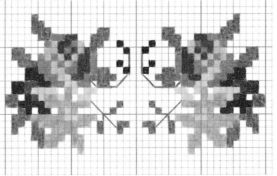

JAPANESE
LIVING ROOM

The imagery and art of Japan has had a profound influence on our lifestyles and our crafts. Many homes include a room decorated in oriental style and this influence is interpreted either through the use of exquisite florals with their unique composition of brushstrokes or the stark minimalism of futons, screens and bold abstract images.

The impact of Japanese costumes, both traditional and theatrical, relies to a large extent on richly illustrated embroideries often depicting flowers and birds. However, for the following projects I have chosen to use lettering and abstract sunrise motifs to fit in with a contemporary living environment.

Japanese Sunrise Bookmark

This simple design could be extended into a runner or place mat by using a fabric with fewer holes to the inch. A larger version worked to the same theme would also have an impact as a window blind (shade).

Actual design measures:
9 × 2¼ in (22.9 × 5.7 cm)

Materials

1 piece of 32-count linen measuring 10½ × 3 in (27 × 7.5 cm)
No 8 crewel needle
1 red bead

Anchor stranded cottons (floss):

 1 skein of red (335)

1 skein of black (403)

Instructions

Mark the centre of your linen and the centre of your chart. Starting here, work the design in cross stitch using two strands of cotton (floss) over two strands of linen. When the design is complete take a 6-in (15.25-cm) length of four strands of black cotton and twist them tightly. Fold them in half to form a twisted cord and thread one end through the bead. Knot to secure. Stitch the other end to the centre back of the two rows of black cross stitch, to form the bottom border. Fray the edges of the linen.

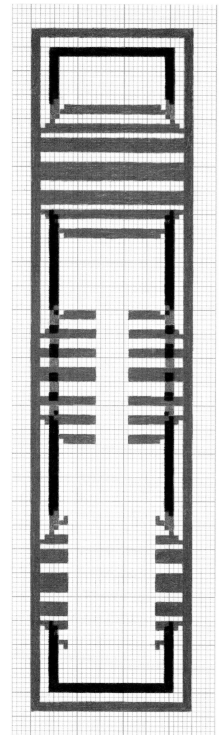

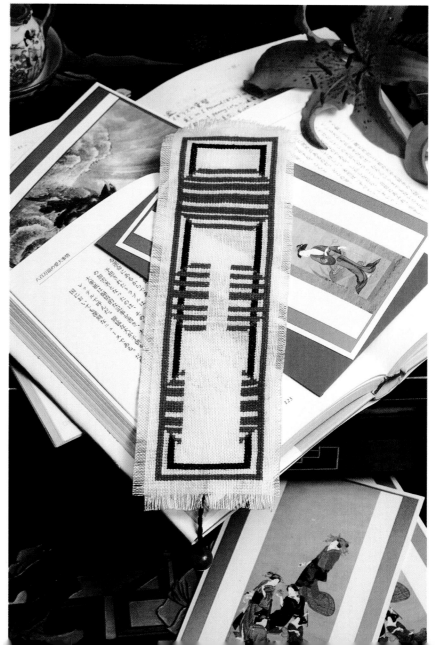

Japanese Paperweight

Blank paperweights provide a useful and interesting showcase for your cross stitch designs and can be bought from many embroidery stores in a variety of shapes and sizes. This circular paperweight works particularly well with my Japanese sun design as the curved glass emphasizes the shape of the sun.

Actual design measures: approximately 2½ in (6.3 cm) square

Materials

1 circular paperweight 3½ in (8.9 cm) in diameter (see stockists/ suppliers information on page 165)
1 piece of 18-count Aida measuring 4 in (10 cm) square
No 8 crewel needle

Anchor stranded cottons (floss):

 1 skein of black (403)
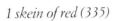 *1 skein of red (335)*

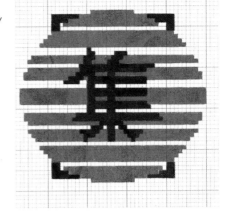

Instructions

Mark the centre of the chart and the centre of the Aida. Starting here, work in cross stitch using two strands of cotton (floss). When the design is complete, cut in a circle using the bottom of the paperweight as a template. Fix according to the manufacturer's instructions.

Japanese Address Book

This is the perfect gift for the man who has everything and it can be adapted to any size of address book. Buy the plain book before you begin and cut your cloth accordingly, working your design in the centre.

Actual design measures:
4½ × 6¾ in (11.5 × 17.1 cm)

Materials

1 piece of 14-count Aida measuring 10 × 13 in (25.4 × 33 cm)
2 strips of heavyweight red cotton measuring 10 × 3 in (25.4 × 7.5 cm)
1 address book measuring 5½ × 8 in (14 × 20.5 cm)
Red sewing thread
No 24 tapestry needle
Rubber-based adhesive

Anchor stranded cottons (floss):

 1 skein of red (335)

 1 skein of white (1)

Instructions

Fold the Aida in half widthways. Mark the centre of your chart and, leaving a 1-in (2.5-cm) selvedge (selvage) on the right edge, centre your design on the right-hand side of the Aida (to the right of the fold).

Using two strands of cotton (floss), work the design entirely in cross stitch. When the embroidery is complete, take your finished canvas and turn in all the edges so it fits exactly over your address book when closed. Using a rubber-based adhesive, glue the top and bottom hems to the back of your work. Take one strip of red cotton fabric and stitch one long edge to the turned back right-hand edge of your worked canvas. Fold back the red fabric to form a flap to hold your book cover, then turn under and stitch the top and bottom edges of red fabric to the top and bottom edges of your canvas. Repeat for the left side. Slip your address book covers into these red flaps.

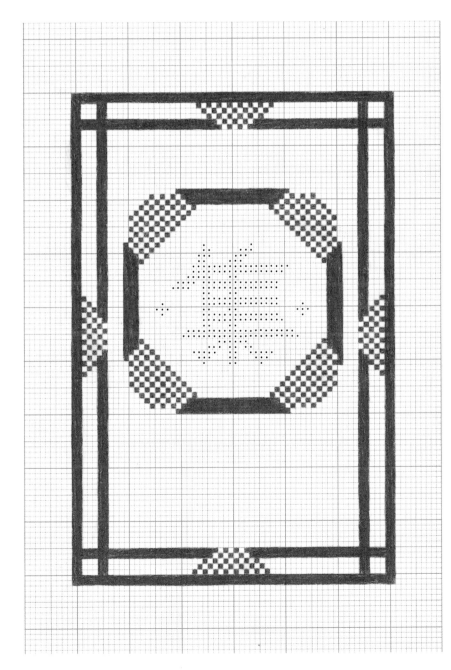

Japanese Lampshade

Lampshades in numerous shapes and sizes can be bought very cheaply from department stores. When selecting a lampshade for embroidery purposes, check that it doesn't have a stiff cardboard or parchment lining. I would also suggest that you do not attempt to embroider the ruched variety which is made from gathered fabric. Also bear in mind that if you work on a light-coloured fine fabric with a dark thread, the back of your stitching may show through when the lamp is turned on. For this reason I have used a lampshade covered in a heavy cotton fabric.

Actual design measures:
5 × 3¾ in (12.7 × 9.5 cm)

Materials

Lampshade
1 piece of 10-count waste canvas
measuring 5 × 6 in
(12.7 × 15.25 cm)
Sewing thread for tacking (basting)
No 7 crewel needle

Anchor Coton à Broder

 2 skeins of black (403)

Instructions

Tack (baste) your waste canvas on to the centre of the lampshade panel that you wish to embroider. Mark the centre of your chart and the centre of your waste canvas and work from here using one strand of Coton à Broder and working in cross stitch throughout over two threads of canvas. Take care not to carry embroidery cotton (floss) across unworked areas at the back of the lampshade as these strands will show through when the lamp is turned on.

When the work is complete, carefully remove the strands of waste canvas from under your embroidery with a pair of tweezers.

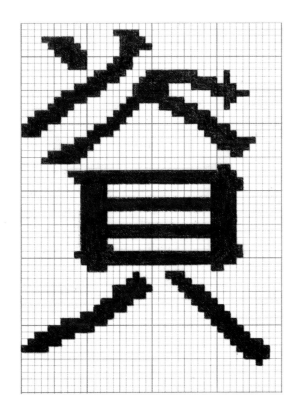

GAMES TABLE
LIVING ROOM

Playing cards, dice, Scrabble tiles and Monopoly boards all provide decorative images that can inspire you. Here are just a few ideas to liven up a card evening but I am sure that you will find many variations of your own. Embroideries based on favourite games make lovely gifts for enthusiasts and, if you take this collection of items as a base, you could also include favourite hobbies in your projects . . . a little bag for golf tees, a folder for cake decorating ideas, key fobs, credit card holders, paperweights . . . look around gift stores and in catalogues for ideas and don't buy it, make it.

Games Tray

Framecraft make a number of different-sized trays especially designed to display your embroidery. You could embroider a square tray in the image of a games board – chess, backgammon or perhaps even Scrabble. If you don't want to buy a tray, why not display your embroidery under the glass top of a coffee table.

Actual design measures:
6½ × 9½ in (16.5 × 24 cm)

Materials
Framecraft tray with oval opening measuring 10¼ × 7¼ in (26.6 × 18.4 cm)
1 piece of 14-count Aida measuring 8½ × 12 in (21.6 × 30.5 cm)
No 24 tapestry needle

Anchor stranded cottons (floss):

3 skeins of blue (131)

1 skein of red (29)

1 skein of black (403)

1 skein of yellow (298)

Instructions
Mark the centre of the chart and the centre of your canvas. Starting here, work the design in cross stitch using three strands of cotton (floss). Work the outline of the cards and the oval in black straight stitches using three strands of cotton. When the design is complete, mount it according to the manufacturer's instructions.

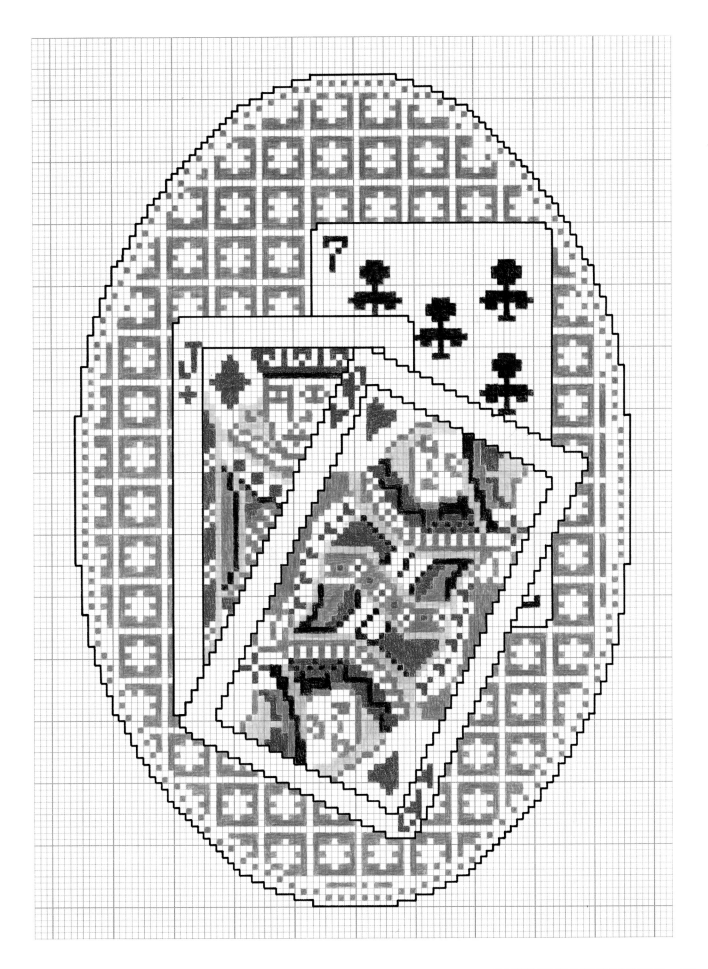

Bridge Pad

This is a neat idea for a bridge pad cover. I have used an ordinary spiral-bound pad, mounted the finished embroidery on cardboard and glued it to the front. When the pad is finished, all you need do is tear off the cover and glue it to the front of the new pad.

Actual design measures:
4¾ × 7 in (12 × 17.8 cm)

Materials
1 piece of 11-count Aida measuring
*   7 × 10 in (17.8 × 25.4 cm)*
1 spiral-bound notepad measuring
*   8 × 5 in (20.5 × 12.7 cm)*
1 piece of cardboard to fit over the
*   front of the notepad*
No 23 tapestry needle
Rubber-based adhesive

Anchor stranded cottons (floss):

◼	*1 skein of blue (131)*
▦	*1 skein of yellow (298)*
▩	*1 skein of red (29)*
◼	*1 skein of black (403)*

Instructions
Mark the centre of the chart and the centre of the canvas. Starting here, work in cross stitch using four strands of cotton (floss). Work the outlines as indicated on the chart in straight stitch using three strands of black cotton (floss). When the embroidery is complete centre it over the cardboard and glue the edges of the canvas to the back. Glue the mounted piece directly on to the front of the notepad.

Playing Card Glasses Case

This project is an example of how you can reduce or enlarge an image by changing the count of the canvas that you work on.

Actual design measures:
6½ × 2¼ in (16.5 × 5.7 cm)

Materials
1 piece of 18-count Aida measuring
*   9 × 4 in (22.9 × 10 cm)*
1 piece of quilted backing fabric
*   measuring 9 × 4 in*
*   (22.9 × 10 cm)*
1 piece of black braid ½ in (12 mm)
*   wide and 4 in (10 cm) long*
No 25 tapestry needle
Black sewing thread

Anchor stranded cottons (floss):

▩	*1 skein of blue (131)*
▦	*1 skein of yellow (298)*
▩	*1 skein of red (29)*
◼	*1 skein of black (403)*

Instructions
Mark the centre of the chart and of the Aida. Starting here, work in cross stitch using two strands of cotton. When the design is complete turn back and tack (baste) the edges, leaving a ½-in (12-mm) border of Aida around the design. Lay the quilted fabric wrong side up. Fold in the right side edges so you have a ¼-in (6-mm) border of fabric visible around all the edges of the Aida. Tack into position. Stitch the Aida to the quilted fabric. Hand stitch the braid across the top of the front panel to finish.

Card Motif Coaster Set

Coasters and paperweights are ideal for cross stitch and can be bought custom-made for the purpose (see the stockists/suppliers on page 165). Alternatively, you can make up your own using glass or Pyrex saucers. Here is how it is done.

Actual design measures: 2½ in (6.3 cm) in diameter

Anchor stranded cottons (floss):

 2 skeins of blue (131)

 1 skein of red (29)

 1 skein of black (403)

Materials

4 glass saucers or coasters with 3-in (7.5-cm) diameter bases
4 circles of cardboard the same size as the saucer bases
4 circles of self-adhesive felt slightly larger than the saucer bases
4 pieces of 18-count Aida measuring 4 in (10 cm) square
No 25 tapestry needle
Rubber-based adhesive
Craft knife

Instructions

Mark the centre of the charts and the centre of each piece of canvas. Starting here, work in cross stitch using two strands of cotton (floss) until the design is complete. Lay the circles of cardboard on the worked Aida and carefully cut the Aida to size. Take the circles of felt, peel off the paper backing and press the wrong side of the embroidery to the centre. Then press the remaining sticky edges of the felt to the bottom of the saucers.

Note: If you have a problem finding self-adhesive felt, buy the clear self-adhesive acetate used for covering books and secure your design to the saucer with this. Kits are available for the coasters and come complete with felt and card (see stockists/suppliers information on page 165).

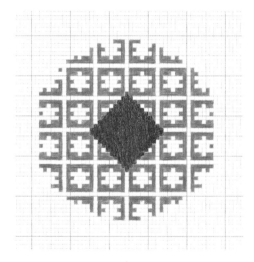
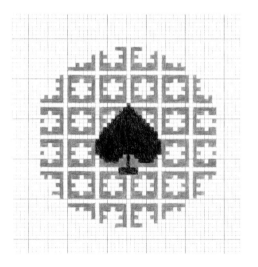
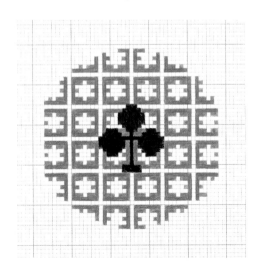

TECHNIQUES

Cross stitch should be a relaxing and therapeutic pastime. For this reason I have no intention of challenging you with complicated instructions or baffling you with brilliant finishing techniques. The object of the exercise is simply to achieve a neatly worked piece of embroidery without bumps and blemishes and to ensure that all your top stitches slope in the same direction. I have indicated alongside the various projects my own approach to making up the specific items. However, there are many other ways of achieving the same results and it really doesn't matter what route you take as long as you are happy with your finished piece of work.

The following information in this section will introduce you to the variety of materials and techniques that you can use in order to transform your design into something special. These materials and guidelines are tried and tested and are those rules that give you the means to produce a professionally finished piece of work of which you can be proud.

Material Facts

The first thing you must decide is what fabric you are going to stitch on. This will be dictated by the size and purpose of your finished item, the intricacy of the design and your chosen threads. I have listed here a selection of traditional needlework fabrics, all of which should be available in any good needlecraft shop.

Custom-made fabrics

Several fabrics are produced especially for cross stitch and make life easier for you because the holes in which you stitch are clearly defined. These are great for beginners. In this category I would recommend Aida or Binca. These are brand names for basket weave fabrics which are available in a range of different counts (stitches per inch), and will enable you to produce a bold, striking pattern or delicate, intricate design with relative ease. The count you select will determine the size of your finished embroidery and will also dictate the thickness of the thread that you can use. The lower the count of the fabric, the fewer stitches per inch it will produce. Binca is widely used in schools and for children's projects because the count is about 6 stitches per inch and it is available in a good range of bright colours. Aida is usually available in 10-18 count in a subtler range of colours.

Evenweave fabrics

Needlecraft shops stock a wide range of what are known as evenweave fabrics. 'Evenweave' means that there are the same number of horizontal and vertical threads in the material, making it easy to count the holes and to make your stitches a uniform size. Once again, you will select your fabric according to the count which is, in

this case, determined by the number of threads you work your cross stitch over.

For example, for fine work you would choose a fabric with a high count and work over one or two threads, while for a bold pattern you would choose a coarser fabric and decide how big you wanted your stitches to be by determining how many threads you were going to work over. Throughout the text in this book I have referred to the measurement of the canvas as count, which refers to the number of holes per inch. Place your measure on a vertical thread of canvas and count how many holes you get in the row for 1 inch. Hardanger and Linda are both attractive evenweave fabrics that can be bought from good needlework stores.

Embroidery linens

These are available in high counts and provide you with a sophisticated background for your work. However, they are expensive, so before selecting them give

consideration to your sight and the time available to you. If you have owlish vision and endless time on your hands, you could produce cross stitch miniatures by working on silk gauze. This can be purchased pre-mounted in a card frame but it really needs to be worked through a magnifying glass: eat lots of carrots before beginning.

Plastic canvas

This is a newcomer to embroidery materials. It is particularly popular with children, has a high count, and can be used for three-dimensional projects such as boxes and toys. You should use wool (yarn), rather than cotton threads, when working with plastic canvas and remember that you will have to fill in your background area. Plastic canvas is fun to work with and your projects will be completed quickly.

Paper canvas

This is a traditional medium which reached its height in popularity during the Victorian era. It is currently enjoying a revival among

---

TOOLS OF THE TRADE

If you are a newcomer to cross stitch you should fill your workbox with the following items:

Small pieces of evenweave and plainweave fabric (see Material Facts below)

Assorted threads

Crewel needles (those with large eyes and sharp points)

Tapestry needles (those with large eyes and blunt points)

Sharp scissors

Waste canvas (see Materials Facts below)

Pencils (plain and transfer)

Tracing paper

A tape measure

Assorted backing fabrics

Polyester wadding (synthetic batting)

Ribbons and laces for trimming

A rubber-based adhesive

A needle threader

A pair of tweezers

Craft (PVA) glue

Medium-weight card

An assortment of sewing threads

stitchers and is used for cut-outs (see Cupid Mirror) and items such as greetings cards, bookmarks and Christmas decorations.

Canvas

This is normally associated with needlepoint rather than cross stitch because it is a coarse, stiff fabric. Standard needlepoint canvases consist of an interlocked single thread (mono canvas) or interlocked double threads (double or Penelope canvas). Both varieties are available in a number of different counts. From 10 count downwards, you should work with wool (yarn) rather than cotton thread.

Specialist embroidery fabrics

These are usually sold by the yard (metre), although you will often require only a very small piece for a project such as a greetings card. For this reason, many needlecraft shops sell bags of scraps, which can be good value.

What you will

Any fabric shop will offer you a vast range of delights on which to embroider designs but most general fabrics are plainweave and are often impossible to count. With a little experience you can safely select cottons with regular patterning such as stripes, ginghams and damasks and gauge your stitch positions according to the printed pattern. Do not attempt to use stretchy or knitted fabrics – your work may pucker. Once again, you must take into account the thickness and weight of your intended yarns before you select your material.

Waste not

Waste canvas is a miraculous invention that makes it possible for you to work on a vast range of materials. It is basically a very loosely woven canvas that is available in a selection of counts. To use it, tack (baste) it to the fabric you wish to work on so that it forms an instant grid that defines the size and position of your stitches to the same extent as Aida. Cross stitch your design in the normal way and then pull out the threads of waste canvas from underneath your embroidery with the help of a pair of tweezers. If you pull out all the vertical threads first, you will find that the horizontal threads virtually fall away by themselves. If you have any problem removing these threads, dampen the fabric and you will find they are easier to remove.

Thread Up

For quality, availability, colour, value and durability I have worked all my designs using Anchor threads. While I have specified particular colour numbers, your finished effect will not be ruined if you go up or down a shade. Stranded cottons (floss) go a long way, especially if you are working on a high count fabric so, after cross stitching for just a short time, you are bound to build up a useful collection of half-used skeins that can be incorporated into future projects.

There is a vast array of threads on the market and your choice will add to the individuality of your work. I have listed a selection of these below and leave it to you to experiment with the different effects and highlights you can achieve. A major consideration should be that all the threads you use in a single project should be of the same thickness. If you mix thicknesses, you will end up with some skimpy crosses and some fat ones which will not be a pretty sight – unless of course, you intend them to look that way.

Stranded cottons (floss)

These are sold in small skeins of 8 metres (approximately 26 ft) containing six individual threads. The idea is that you cut a workable length – about 20 in (50 cm) – and split the threads so that you have as many strands as you need for your particular fabric. You can of course mix strands of several colours together to give a subtle shaded effect and you can buy skeins that are already shaded.

Coton à broder

This is a flat unmercerized thread which works well in bolder designs. It comes in a good range of colours but does pick up the dust more easily than the slightly shiny varieties. Danish and German flower threads are also flat cottons (floss) but are finer. All are spun as a single thread and are not designed to be separated or stranded. They impart a lovely soft quality to your work.

Silks

Stranded cottons (floss) are mercerized and therefore have a pleasantly silky lustre. However, for the perfectionists among us, there is nothing like the real thing. Silk is available in stranded form and in twisted threads. It is expensive and not very easy to work with because the delicate fibres snag on rough skin. However, the finished effect on very fine work is quite special . . . reserve it for your masterpiece.

Pearl cottons

Pearl cotton (coton perlé) is a single-twist, high-lustre thread that comes in a good selection of colours, including some with a shaded effect. It is available in three different weights, which you choose from according to your background fabric.

Fancies

In addition to the above, fancy threads, including a wonderful range of metallics by Kreinik, are constantly being introduced. These can be used to great effect for highlighting details but be sure to check that the thickness of the thread will marry with the basic threads you have chosen.

Get Organized

If you are anything like me you will always pull the wrong loose end on a skein of thread and end up with a knotted mess that will prove a great joy to your cat. To avoid this, it is a good idea to make yourself a thread organizer before beginning a project. All you need is a small strip of lightweight cardboard (an old greetings card is ideal) and a hole punch. Make a hole for each colour down the right-hand side of the card and cut your thread into manageable lengths – 20 in (50 cm) is fine. Next to the relevant hole write the colour number and, if appropriate, the symbol on the chart, and loop your lengths of thread through it. You can then easily pull out the thread as and when you need it.

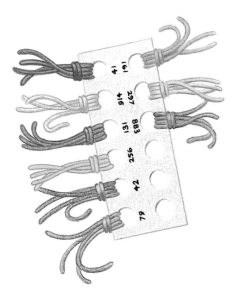

A thread organizer.

Get the Needle

To work cross stitch on evenweave fabrics, use a blunt-ended tapestry needle. To work using waste canvas you need a selection of crewel needles with sharp points and long, flat eyes that allow you to thread a number of strands through at one time without damaging the fabric.

Needles are available in various sizes, and the size you use will depend on the fabric count and the number of strands you are using. A suggested size is given with each project but, as a rule of thumb, use one that feels comfortable and travels easily through your fabric.

Embroidery Frames

When I am working with an evenweave fabric such as Aida, I do not consider it necessary to use a frame. However, I always use a frame when I am stitching on plainweave fabrics or working on a very large project.

There are various types of frames on the market, and the most popular for cross stitch is the hoop, which consists of two concentric circles, one of which is laid under your work and the other laid over your work and then tightened with a screw to hold the fabric taut. It is a good idea to bind both rings with masking tape before beginning because the hoop may mark or distort delicate fabrics.

The other most popular type of frame consists of two parallel dowels with webbing on to which you tack (baste) the opposite ends of your fabric. The dowels are then slotted into two straight uprights, which can be tightened to hold the dowels securely. You can rotate the dowels to move the fabric up and down to keep it taut.

Light Up

One miracle of modern science that I would not be without is the daylight bulb. Given that most of us are busy people who only have the evenings available to stitch in, good lighting, especially when you are counting stitches, is essential. Daylight bulbs ease the strain and can be combined with a custom-made magnifying lamp on an adjustable stand, all of which makes stitching comfortable and pleasurable. (See the stockists/suppliers information on page 165.) You can also buy special holders for your charts and no end of other paraphernalia that will help you to get the job done and take the strain out of your work.

Charts

Many people are frightened of charts, but all you need to remember is that every coloured square represents one complete stitch. The heavier lines on the grid are put there to make counting easier for you because each block of squares between the heavy lines represents 10 stitches. Your colour key gives you the correct colour-coded thread to use so you really cannot go wrong. If you find that you get lost on a chart the best solution is to take a photocopy of it and cross off the squares as you work them. I work in blocks of colour rather than rows and I keep a number of needles threaded with the different shades of thread so I can change from one to another as necessary.

Sizing the Design

For almost every design in this book I give the actual size of the motif that you will achieve if you work on my recommended background fabric. However, it is quite easy to re-size the motif by changing the count of the fabric you use. There is a simple formula for working out the size of your design

– let's take the games tray design as an example. First, count the number of stitches across at the widest point; on this chart it is 92 stitches. Now count the number of stitches vertically; it is 134. If you were going to work this design on 28-count linen over two threads, you would need to halve the count to determine the number of stitches to the inch. On 28-count linen you would achieve 14 stitches to the inch. You should now divide the number of stitches on your chart by the number of stitches to the inch – that is (width) 92 stitches divided by 14 = 6.57 in (about 17 cm) × (height) 134 stitches divided by 14 = 9.57 in (about 24.5 cm).

When you are working on Aida, or over one thread of fabric, do not halve the count before dividing. When calculating how much fabric you need, remember to add at least 1 in (2.5 cm) of extra fabric on all sides of each project to allow for backing or, if it is a picture, for mounting.

If you want to re-size a design in a major way, your best approach is with a hand-drawn grid. First, trace the outline of your design and draw a squared grid over it. Draw a second grid to the size you require

and copy the design square by square from one to the other. Place the enlarged version over a sheet of graph paper and fill in the symbols within the traced outlines. This approach should also be used when copying designs from fabric or china (see the Mix and Match section).

Charting paper is now available in clear acetate which you place over any image that you wish to chart and fill in the symbols. Alternatively, you can enlarge your design with the use of a photocopier and then re-define the grid by drawing in extra crossed lines to fill in with symbols.

Another method of enlarging is to read every symbol on the chart as a block of four stitches. This in principle will double the size of your design, although you may find it necessary to round off corners by taking away or adding a few stitches at the edges as you work.

Transferring Designs

If you do not wish to work with waste canvas you can easily transfer the image with a water-erasable transfer pencil (available from needlework shops and haberdashers/notions departments)

and tracing paper. First, test your fabric by drawing a cross on the tracing paper. Place this face down on the fabric and press it with a warm iron. If this takes to the fabric, you can then trace your complete design and transfer it. There are some wonderful colour transfer pens and paints on the market, so you could trace or paint the design in full colour and then transfer it to the fabric by ironing it on.

Centring Designs

Throughout the book I have suggested that you find the centre of the fabric before beginning your embroidery. There are various methods of doing this. If you are using Aida you can count the holes vertically and horizontally and halve the totals to find the centre. You could use a tape measure and halve the measurement or you can fold your fabric both horizontally and vertically to establish the centre point. When you are establishing the centre point on a piece of fabric that has more selvedge (selvage) on one side than the other, start your count or measurement after the selvedge line.

To find the centre of the charts,

Cross stitch on plainweave fabric.

Cross stitch on evenweave fabric (Aida)

count the stitches and halve the total. If there is no stitch at the centre point, count out to the nearest stitch and start on the equivalent position on your fabric. On establishing your central point you might find it useful to tack (baste) a line of stitches both horizontally and vertically on your fabric as a guide. Always work out from the centre unless the instructions specify otherwise.

Getting Started

Before beginning your work, prevent potential disasters by making sure of the following:

1 Your hands are spotlessly clean and do not smell of garlic. They will need regular washing as fabrics and threads pick up the dirt very easily.

2 Your tea or coffee is at a safe distance from your work and that delicious chocolate cake with the gooey icing is not sitting there tempting you to pick it up.

3 The animals have all been instructed not to sit on your lap/shoulder/head and have learned to wipe their paws before coming in from the garden and climbing all over you.

4 The children are doing their painting somewhere else.

5 No one or nothing within reach of you is moulting.

Stitching

Remember the first rule of cross stitch – that all the top stitches slope in the same direction. This can be achieved either by working a row of bottom stitches in one direction and then coming back along the row in the opposite direction or by working each complete cross individually. Both these methods are perfectly acceptable but the option you choose should depend on how many stitches you have in a row before the colour changes. You can work in any direction, but always insert your needle after the correct number of threads in your background material. The diagrams show a cross stitch being worked over two threads on both plainweave fabric and the position of your stitch on evenweave fabric. It is a good idea to thread several needles with different colours before you begin. Use a needle threader – it will save your sight and a great deal of time.

Cross stitch is the only stitch you need to master to complete the majority of projects in this book. However, one or two of the designs require additional stitches. When I refer to straight stitch I mean exactly that: small, back stitches worked in a row, the same size as a half cross stitch. Half stitch is as it sounds, work the first half of a cross stitch only, ie do not go back to complete the full cross. I have also used star stitch on the Shell Make-up Bag (see page 80).

Stretching

I did not find it necessary to block any of the projects in this book. However, if you do find the shape of your work is slightly distorted, place it face down on a sheet of board, which you should cover with clean paper or a sheet, and pull it into shape by inserting tacks at 1 in (2.5 cm) intervals. Dampen your work with a clean sponge or spray and leave it to dry.

Framing

Because cross stitch fabric is very soft it is usually quite simple when you are framing projects to stretch your finished work into shape on a backing board and either glue it into position using a rubber-based adhesive or, using strong string, lace it across the back in criss-cross fashion until it is taut (see diagram).

To frame your cross stitch, centre your finished work on a sheet of cardboard and insert all the way round at 1 in (2.5 cm) intervals. Then either glue in into position or lace it across the back with string, as shown here.

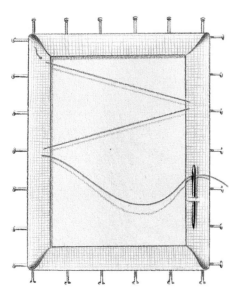

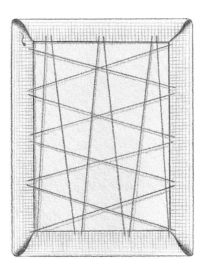

MAKING A CROCHET CHAIN

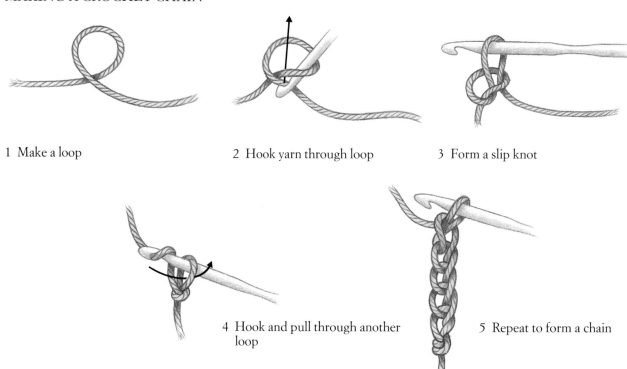

1 Make a loop

2 Hook yarn through loop

3 Form a slip knot

4 Hook and pull through another loop

5 Repeat to form a chain

Before using either of these methods, centre your finished work on your card and insert pins, starting with the four corners and then spaced at 1 in (2.5 cm) intervals all around the edge of the needlework and card to ensure it is straight and undistorted. You can then add a decorative mount to the front or frame it in whichever fashion you please. Finished pieces intended for book covers and folders can be pulled into shape during the finishing process. When mounting a piece of embroidery, use acid-free board to ensure it remains in good condition for the generations ahead of you who will treasure your work.

Trimmings
I hope this book has given you lots of new ideas for ways to use your cross stitch projects. Most craft people are, by nature, collectors and I would expect you to have a basket or box of fabric pieces and

furnishing trims. Use whatever you fancy to make a project, but take into account the weight of any fabric you intend using against the weight of the material you have cross stitched on. In a couple of projects I have used twisted cords and crochet chains as edgings and fastenings.

To make a twisted cord, hold several strands of cotton (floss) together and tie one end to something solid. Repeatedly twist this length of thread until it is tight and then, keeping the twist, unfasten the tied end. Hold both ends together and let the doubled cord twist around itself. Secure at both ends.

To make a crochet chain, follow the step-by-step diagrams above.

Aftercare
However careful you are, accidents inevitably happen but if you have used the recommended threads you should have no problem repairing

the damage. Before washing a piece of embroidery always check the colour fastness of the thread and fabric you have used and follow the manufacturer's instructions. Anchor threads are reputed to be fast-dyed and can be machine washed at 96°F (35°C) but you must also take the instructions for washing the background fabric into account. As a general rule, avoid bleach and biological powders and do not tumble-dry. When you iron your work, place it face down over a fluffy towel to prevent any flattening of the stitches. Then steam press or use a damp cloth, ironing on the wrong side of the work only.

Stockists (Suppliers) Information

Many of the lace and cotton items featured in this book are available as complete embroidery kits by mail order. For full details contact the following:

Melinda Coss
Ty'r Waun Bach
Gwernogle
Dyfed
West Wales SA32 7RY
United Kingdom
Tel and fax: (0267) 202 386 (office hours only please)

For details of the items listed below contact:

Framecraft Miniatures Ltd
148–150 High Street
Aston
Birmingham B6 4US
United Kingdom

Ann Brinkley Designs
761 Palmer Avenue
Holmdel
NJ 97733
United States

Gay Bowles
PO Box 1060
Janesville
WI 53547
United States

Candle screen page 100; Collector's Cabinet page 91; Paperweight page 145; Games Tray page 152; Coasters page 156; Brush, Mirror and Comb Set page 99; Linen Towel page 103; Door Plate page 64; Bell Pull page 136; Grow Chart fixtures page 56.

Anchor cottons (floss), Kreinik Metallics, Aida fabrics and ready-to-sew accessories, including the Pot Holder (page 17) and the

Shell Guest Towel (page 79) were kindly supplied by the following companies. Write to them for details of local stockists.

Coats Patons Crafts
PO Box McMullen Road
Darlington
County Durham DL1 1YO
United Kingdom

Coats & Clark Inc
30 Patewood Drive
Suite 351
Greenville
South Carolina 29615
United States

Kreinik Manufacturing Co Inc
9199 Reistertown Road
Suite 209B
Owings Mills MD 21117
United States

Daylight bulbs and magnifying lamps are available from:

Daylight Studios
223a Portobello Road
London W11 1LU
United Kingdom

Transfer pens, paints, needlework fabrics and much more are available from:

Atlascraft Ltd
Ludlow Hill Road
Melton Road
West Bridgford
Nottingham NG2 6HD
United Kingdom

For details of ribbon stockists contact:

Offray Ribbon
Fir Tree Place
Church Road
Ashford
Middlesex TW15 2PH
United Kingdom

The author would also like to recommend the following company for their wonderful graphic and special effect pens:

C W Edding (UK) Ltd
Edding House
Merlin Centre
Acrewood Way
St Albans
Hertfordshire AL4 0JY
United Kingdom

Conversion Chart									
Anchor	DMC	Anchor	DMC	Anchor	DMC	Anchor	DMC	Anchor	DMC
1	White (blanc)	85	3609	205	912	295	727	667	841
		89	718	227	701	298	725	681	730
10	351	97	553	229	699	304	741	843	3053
13	817	99	552	231	453	305	743	849	3752
19	326	101	550	233	451	326	900	861	3051
23	963	109	210	234	762	330	3340	868	3779
24	776	117	341	235	414	334	606	892	225
25	3708	118	340	255	907	335	606	893	224
26	894	119	333	256	906	362	437	894	223
27	893	128	800	258	905	374	841	895	223
28	892	130	809	265	3348	386	746	903	611
29	891	131	798	266	3347	397	762	925	970
54	956	159	827	279	834	398	415	928	3761
55	604	167	519	291	444	403	310	936	632
57	602	168	518	292	3078	410	995	Kreinik	–
77	3687	203	954	293	727	4146	754	Silver	

Acknowledgements

The author would like to provide all
the following people with luxury
cruises, diamond tiaras, crates of
champagne and cases of caviar.
As she currently has prior obligations
relating to the feeding of her cats,
chickens and poodle, she hopes her
sincerest thanks will be enough.

For making this book possible
through their excellent and
endless stitching:
Coral Gibson,
Carolyn Palmer,
Anne Peterson,
Valerie Clark,
Freda Brown and
Audrey Bonnaud.

For turning the needlework into
lovely things:
Jeanette Hall.

For exceeding herself, yet again,
with her wonderful photography:
Di Lewis.

For nervous breakdown prevention,
my editors:
Jane Donovan and
Jane Struthers.

For encouragement and support:
Carey Smith and
Colin Gower.

For their help and friendship:
Pat Groves and
Lydia Darbyshire.

The publishers would like to thank the following for their kind help in
loaning objects for photography:
Ray Coggins Antiques, Westbury, Wiltshire.
David Plagerson, Totnes, Devon.
Fosse Farmhouse, Nettleford, Near Chippenham, Wiltshire.

Index